Wake Tech. Libraries
9101 Fayetteville Road
Raleigh, North Carolina 27603-5696

WITHDRAWN

The Origins of the Literary Vampire

The Origins of the Literary Vampire

Heide Crawford

ROWMAN & LITTLEFIELD
Lanham • Boulder • New York • London

Published by Rowman & Littlefield
A wholly owned subsidiary of The Rowman & Littlefield Publishing Group, Inc.
4501 Forbes Boulevard, Suite 200, Lanham, Maryland 20706
www.rowman.com

Unit A, Whitacre Mews, 26-34 Stannary Street, London SE11 4AB

Copyright © 2016 by Rowman & Littlefield

All rights reserved. No part of this book may be reproduced in any form or by any electronic or mechanical means, including information storage and retrieval systems, without written permission from the publisher, except by a reviewer who may quote passages in a review.

British Library Cataloguing in Publication Information Available

Library of Congress Cataloging-in-Publication Data

Names: Crawford, Heide, 1966– author.
Title: The origins of the literary vampire / Heide Crawford.
Description: Lanham : Rowman & Littlefield, 2016. | Includes bibliographical references and index.
Identifiers: LCCN 2016013549 (print) | LCCN 2016026582 (ebook) | ISBN 9781442266742 (cloth : alk. paper) | ISBN 9781442266759 (electronic)
Subjects: LCSH: Vampires in literature. | German literature—History and criticism. | Vampires—Europe, Central—History.
Classification: LCC PT148.V3 C73 2016 (print) | LCC PT148.V3 (ebook) | DDC 830.9/375—dc23
LC record available at https://lccn.loc.gov/2016013549

∞ ™ The paper used in this publication meets the minimum requirements of American National Standard for Information Sciences Permanence of Paper for Printed Library Materials, ANSI/NISO Z39.48-1992.

Printed in the United States of America

To the believers

Contents

Acknowledgments — ix

Introduction: Germany's Place in the History of the Vampire in Literature — xi

1. The Habsburgs, Vampires, and Scientific Inquiry: The Vampire's Path to Literature — 1
2. The First Vampire Poems — 21
3. The First German Vampire Stories — 73
4. The Development of a Horror Aesthetic by German Poets — 103

Appendix: Vampire Poems — 109

Works Cited — 121

Index — 125

About the Author — 129

Acknowledgments

Vampires, ghosts, witches, and zombies bring people together, especially if these people share an academic fondness for the art of writing horror and fear. Some of the people who have inspired, influenced, and supported me are Markus Winkler, Tom Beebee, and my dear friend and mentor Maria Carlson, who has always been a great believer in and supporter of this project. It is especially gratifying to have a friend to meet up with to discuss monsters on a regular basis. I love our time together, Manya. Philip Simpson, Mary Findley, Brad Duren, Carl Sederholm, Marcus Mallard—my colleagues and friends in all things vampire and zombie—where would I be without the numerous invigorating discussions on panels and roundtables at the Popular Culture Association's conferences over the years? I am also especially grateful to the *Deutsches Literaturarchiv* in Marbach, Germany, and the *Deutsches Volksliedarchiv* in Freiburg, Germany for their assistance with my research. And last but certainly not least, my family's quiet patience and trust that this book would be written was just the support I needed. My thanks and love go out to my husband Troy in particular, because his confidence in this project never waned, though mine often did.

Introduction

Germany's Place in the History of the Vampire in Literature

All nations have their omens drear,
Their legends wild of woe and fear.—Sir Walter Scott

Cursed to rise from the grave and suck the blood of the living, the vampire has haunted graveyards, ancient castles, dark alleys, and our collective imaginations since time immeasurable. He has been dashing, mysterious, intriguing, and dangerous, with exotic eastern European elegance and the requisite distinctive accent. He has beguiled men and seduced women, only to drain them of their vitality, sustaining himself on the warm, rich blood in an effort to live forever. Indeed, this irresistible and alluring monster refuses to die. Since the eighteenth century, poets, philosophers, scientists, anthropologists, medical doctors, literary scholars, filmmakers, and at least one emperor have unearthed this monster from the dusty tombs of folklore and superstition for academic study and for creative use. The vampire has even adapted quite well to the late twentieth and early twenty-first centuries in popular television series and computer games. Poets have re-imagined this monster from superstition time and time again, and over the centuries they have added new traits to an already multifaceted monster. Similarly, scholars have continued to investigate the vampire phenomenon in literature, film, and popular culture in an effort to explain its popular appeal, how and why it evolved, and what it can represent as a literary figure. Numerous studies seek to interpret the symbolic value of the vampire in literature and film, its history and its aesthetic value, thus keeping it alive. After so many new adaptations of the vampire in the arts and interpretations of it in scholarship since its inception in literature in the eighteenth century, many questions about its origins and manifestations in literature, art, and film arise. This study aims to offer some clarification by addressing the origins of the literary vampire in German literature during the eighteenth century, and the influence of German poets on the development of the literary vampire in particular and Gothic horror literature in general.

The long and illustrious tradition of the literary vampire begins in Germany in the mid-eighteenth century, when German poets first adapted the vampire figure from central European folklore and superstition for use in their works. Despite these German beginnings, scholarly attention devoted to literary vampires has consistently focused on a select set of sources: British and French literature, Bram Stoker's Dracula, and the phenomenon of the vampire superstition in general. While there are many studies of folkloric vampires and literary vampires, the story of the crucial moment of transition from folkloric monster to literary figure has not yet been told. This book aims to tell this story by tracing the development of the literary vampire from its first appearance in literature with the German poem, "Der Vampir," by Heinrich August Ossenfelder in 1748, to its introduction into prose by German authors in the early nineteenth century. In their appropriations of the vampire for their creative work, German poets were informed primarily by central European vampire stories that circulated throughout Europe in the beginning of the eighteenth century, largely due to Austrian Emperor Charles VI's efforts to study this strange superstition that prevailed in the territories that he had recently acquired in wars against the Turks. However, in addition to giving the first German vampires the basic traits from the central European vampire tradition, German poets added new traits to the literary vampire by connecting it with specific motifs, such as the *femme fatale* and the "dead lover returns," that modern readers automatically associate with the vampire, some of which are also connected with Germany's own folkloric vampire tradition. An understanding of the literary vampire's origins in German literature, of its connection to the central European vampire stories collected for Charles VI, and of the degree to which German poets' adaptations of the vampire were also informed by Germany's own vampire folklore provides a comprehensive image of the literary vampire in its cultural-historical context.

GERMANY'S PLACE IN THE GOTHIC TRADITION

German authors played an important role in the development of Gothic horror literature, beginning with the publication and immediate international success of Gottfried August Bürger's ballad, "Lenore," in 1774.[1] As Neil Cornwell suggests in his chapter on the "European Gothic" in David Punter's volume, *A Companion to the Gothic* (2000), Bürger's ballad was significant, not only for its popular appeal, but especially because it contributed the classic Gothic image of the "revenant bridegroom" to the genre (Cornwell 2000, 31). Ludwig Tieck, Heinrich von Kleist, and E. T. A. Hoffmann also profoundly influenced the development of European Gothic horror in the nineteenth century. Hoffmann in particular inspired many of the greatest European and American writers of Gothic horror fiction, including Edgar Allan Poe, Gérard de Nerval, Nikolai Gogol, and Fyodor Dostoevsky, whose works "would seem inconceivable without Hoffmann" (Cornwell 2000, 33). Friedrich Schiller's wildly popular fragmentary Gothic novel, *Der Geisterseher* (1787–1789), though not a vampire tale, inspired Lord Byron's work and greatly influenced Samuel Taylor Coleridge, Charles Maturin, and Charles Brockden Brown, to name a few (Cornwell 2000, 32; Lloyd-Smith 2000, 111). As a genre, Gothic horror literature reflected many of the "political, social, cultural and religious anxieties of the eighteenth century [that] were felt Europe-wide" (Cornwell 2000, 27). In order to express these anxieties, authors of Gothic horror literature combined opposing forces in society, such as life and death, love and fear, imprisonment and freedom, sexual repression and lust, in narratives that were shrouded in an aura of mystery, often suggesting a supernatural element. The literary vampire is the embodiment of these opposing realities and passions that are reflective of the human condition, and the concentration of such strong, contrasting emotions in one horrific body creates an atmosphere of sublime Gothic horror in the earliest German vampire literature. Even before Horace Walpole wrote his programmatic Gothic novel, *The Castle of Otranto* in 1764, the German literary vampire, created by Ossenfelder, represented these elements of Gothic horror.

DEFINING THE VAMPIRE

Any discussion of the vampire should offer a working definition of this monster, especially as it compares to other similar figures in literature. A commonly held definition of the vampire is reproduced by the German scholar of British literature, Aribert Schroeder, in his book *Vampirismus: Seine Entwicklung vom Thema zum Motiv* (1973):

> Beim Vampirismus handelt es sich, allgemein gesehen, um einen Aberglauben, bei dem es um Wesen geht, die Menschen und Tieren das Blut aussaugen und sie auf diese Weise töten. (5)
> (Generally speaking, vampirism is a superstition about beings who suck the blood of people and animals and kill them in this manner. [my translation])

This definition is included here in order to demonstrate the simplicity with which a very complex character is often defined. We will see, however, that this definition is too restrictive, especially with regard to the original vampire stories that influenced German poets. Interestingly, this initial definition is even too simplistic for Schroeder. Based on his analysis of a variety of descriptions from several doctors, scientists, and commanding officers under Emperor Charles VI who wrote treatises on the vampire phenomenon in the early decades of the eighteenth century, Schroeder expands on his initial definition of the vampire with the following:

> Bei einem Vampir handelt es sich um einen Toten, der nachts sein Grab verläßt, um seinen Opfern das Blut auszusaugen. Er greift Menschen und Tiere an. Tagsüber muß er in seinem Grabe liegen, an das er gebunden ist. Der Leichnam eines Vampirs zeigt keine oder geringfügige Zeichen von Verwesung. Auf Leben in ihm deuten seine frische Gesichtsfarbe, Laute, die er von sich gibt und andere Zeichen. Manchmal läuft ihm das Blut seiner Opfer aus Mund, Nase und Ohren oder es verändert seinen Körperumfang. Ein Vampir ist besonders gefährlich, weil seine Opfer ebenfalls Vampire werden müssen, sobald sie gestorben sind. (1973, 7)
> (A vampire is a dead person who leaves his grave at night to suck the blood of his victims. He attacks people and animals. During the day he must lie in his grave, to which he is bound. The body of a vampire shows no signs of decomposition, or the signs are insignificant. Signs of life include a fresh complexion, sounds that he emits and others. Sometimes blood from his victims runs from his mouth, nose and ears or the blood alters his body's shape. A vampire is especially dangerous, because his victims must also become vampires as soon as they have died. [my translation])

However inclusive this second approach at a definition of the vampire at first appears, it is a definition that is informed by literary adaptations of the vampire rather than by the vampire from folklore. The folkloric vampire did not always drink blood, and his general appearance and demeanor varied from country to country where these tales were told.[2]

Schroeder's definition also fails to include the ambiguous nature of the folkloric vampire as a ghost-like phenomenon that robs its victims of their vitality, which is essential for the analysis of influential vampire folktales and the first German vampire poems and prose works. In fact, folklorists have used the terms "vampire," "ghost," and "revenant" interchangeably. For example, one folktale that will be addressed in the next chapter, "The Shoemaker of Silesia," refers to the revenant as a ghost, even though he does not appear as a disembodied spirit, but rather in the flesh. The first use of the word "vampire" in the *Oxford English Dictionary* of 1734 defines vampires as "evil spirits [who animate the] bodies of deceased persons" (quoted in Auerbach 1995, 20). In his book *The Vampire*, Montague Summers distinguishes the vampire from the ghost and the demon by mentioning that, unlike the vampire, the demon possesses a body other than his own, and the ghost returns to the world of the living as an intangible spirit (2). My own working definition of the vampire is a corporeal revenant that rises from its grave, causes harm to or kills its victims, to whom it is immediately recognizable as a deceased loved one or simply as human, and returns to its grave. The clearest distinction between the vampire and the ghost is that the vampire is immediately recognizable to its victims as the returned, reanimated corpse of the deceased rather than as the deceased's returned spirit. It should already be clear from the above attempts that definitions of the vampire are varied and dependent on the particular regional folklore under investigation. This is also true for German poets' conceptions of the vampire when they included it as a figure in their creative work.

THE VAMPIRE METAPHOR

Once a clear connection has been established between the first literary representations of vampires by German poets and the folklore that informed them in this process, it is important to understand the metaphorical significance that the poets gave the monster for their creative work. In the chapters that address these first literary adaptations of the vampire, I base my analysis on theories of horror literature and the literary monster put forth by Noël Carroll in his book, *The Philosophy of Horror or Paradoxes of the Heart* (1990), and by Jeffrey Jerome Cohen in his book, *Monster Theory: Reading Culture* (1996), respectively. Carroll makes the observations that "the horror genre is a means through which the anxieties of an era can be expressed" and that "the horror genre is capable of incorporating or assimilating general social anxieties into its iconography of fear and distress" (Carroll 1990, 207). Cohen's monster theory reflects these ideas when he suggests that the monster embodies the fears and anxieties of the culture that produces it, essentially functioning in this way as a "cultural body" when its body "quite literally incorporates fear, desire, anxiety and fantasy . . . giving them life and an uncanny independence. The monstrous body is pure culture" (Cohen 1996, 4). As we will see, the vampires in the first German poems and prose works typically reflect a variety of social fears, anxieties, and taboos in their physical and personality traits and in their interactions with the mortals they encounter. In sum, my analyses of the first vampire poems and prose works by German poets will focus on their connections to central European and German vampire folklore, their significance as metaphors for social anxieties, taboos, and fears, and the various traits these poets added to the image of the literary vampire that have become commonplace in modern horror literature.

THE LITERARY VAMPIRE'S ORIGINS

Direct connections between the central European vampire stories and the literary vampire are evident in Ossenfelder's poem when he mentions place names taken directly from a central European vampire story, and in Hoffmann's story, "Vampirismus," when the storytellers in the frame narrative discuss one of the reports of vampires collected for Charles VI. This necessitates a closer look at the cultural history of central European vampire folklore as it became relevant for eighteenth-century poets in Germany, which is the focus of chapter 1. Specifically, the focus of the chapter is on the Habsburg Emperor Charles VI's initiatives to commission anthropological and scientific investigations to his newly acquired lands in Hungary after his victory over the Ottoman Turks in the Turkish War (1716–1718) and the documentation of indigenous people's customs, based on a fear of vampirism, of exhuming their dead. The emphasis here is on the folktales and reports that inspired the publication of the first vampire poem in the popular scientific journal, *Der Naturforscher* (*The Natural Scientist*), in 1748. Folksongs collected at the German Folklore Archive in Freiburg, Germany, show that Germany's own folkloric tradition of vampires or vampire-like monsters did not inform the creation of the literary vampire by German poets entirely. Instead, some traits from German folksongs and especially from the European Lenore legend were very likely used by German authors to embellish some of the vampire traits they derived from the central European vampire stories. By comparing German vampire folklore with that of central Europe, I argue that while German poets adopted for their literary vampires some features from local traditions of zombie-like vampires that chewed on themselves in their graves (*Nachzehrer*), and likewise took on the necrophilic undertones suggested by the Lenore legend, they were primarily influenced by the central European vampire figures.

Chapter 2 addresses the first vampires in German poetry in chronological order: Heinrich August Ossenfelder's poem, "Der Vampir"; Gottfried August Bürger's poem, "Lenore" (1774); Johann Wolfgang Goethe's poem, "Die Braut von Korinth" (The Bride of Corinth, 1797); and two poems by Joseph von Eichendorff, "Das kalte Liebchen" (The Cold Sweetheart, 1816) and "Die späte Hochzeit" (The Late Wedding, 1828). The focus in the analyses of these poems is on their cultural-historical context and the motifs that German poets connected with the vampire, which would subsequently become definitive for the literary vampire and for Gothic horror fiction in the nineteenth century and beyond.

The third chapter focuses on the first German vampire prose works that were written in the beginning of the nineteenth century and the contributions they made to the development of the literary vampire and Gothic horror literature. These vampire stories by German authors are Ludwig Tieck's

"Liebeszauber" (Love Magic, 1812); E. T. A. Hoffmann's "Vampirismus" (Vampirism, 1821), which is part of his collection of stories, *Die Serapionsbrüder* (1819–1821); Ernst Benjamin Salomo Raupach's "Laßt die Todten ruhen" (Wake Not the Dead, 1823); the first known German vampire novel, *Der Vampir oder die Todtenbraut* (The Vampire, or the Dead Bride, 1828), by Theodor Hildebrandt; and the novella *Der Fremde* (The Mysterious Stranger, 1847) by Karl Adolf von Wachsmann. The story by Raupach is known to English-speaking readers of Gothic horror fiction in its English translation, "Wake Not the Dead," or by its alternate title, "The Bride of the Grave"; it has been falsely attributed to Ludwig Tieck by many scholars, since Peter Haining published his collection of Gothic horror stories, *Gothic Tales of Terror*, in 1973.

This study of the origins of the literary vampire in German literature concludes with a discussion of the broad international impact that German poets' adaptations of the vampire figure had for the development of Gothic horror literature and the conceptualization of an aesthetic of horror for future generations of authors and filmmakers. Despite their varied contributions to the development of Gothic horror literature, German authors' stories are unique in their reluctance to offer a final explanation for the Gothic horror they present. This is in contrast to the common model of British Gothic horror literature, in which the horror, mystery, and supernatural elements in the story are often explained in the end, a feature known as the "explained supernatural" and usually associated with Ann Radcliffe's novels. In German Gothic horror tales, however, mysterious events and supernatural occurrences are not always explained, at least not in a satisfactory manner for the reader, and nobody lives happily ever after; in fact, the protagonists usually die or they go insane. The achieved—and intended—effect of this common German narrative style that leads the reader along the same uncertain path as the protagonist without the luxury of clarity is one of limitless horror. The everlasting horror in the German stories may explain their international popular appeal, especially among British readers toward the end of the eighteenth century. Contemporary British readers probably identified easily with Isabella's excitement when she recommends a long list of "horrid" stories to her friend, Catherine, many of which are German or at least set in Germany, in Jane Austen's novel *Northanger Abbey* (Austen 1995, 39). Either that or they laughed along with Austen at the virtual plague of horror stories coming out of Germany, many of which featured vampires, all of which contributed in one way or another to the development of European Gothic horror literature and the image we have today of its favorite monster: the vampire.

NOTES

1. The translation of Bürger's poem into English in 1796 was Sir Walter Scott's first publication.

2. The belief that vampires suck blood comes from observations of blood at the mouth of the alleged vampire by those who exhumed the body. This is a natural part of decomposition caused by the pooling of blood in the body cavity. Blood tends to appear at the mouth most often when the alleged vampire has been buried face down, a common practice if the deceased was expected to become a vampire (Barber 2010, 115).

Chapter One

The Habsburgs, Vampires, and Scientific Inquiry

The Vampire's Path to Literature

> *If there is in this world a well-attested account, it is that of the vampires. Nothing is lacking: official reports, affidavits of well-known people, of surgeons, of priests, of magistrates; the judicial proof is most complete. And with all that, who is there who believes in vampires?*—Jean-Jacques Rousseau, Lettre à l'Archevêque de Paris

In his book *The Philosophy of Horror* (1990), Noël Carroll argues that horror, whether in literature or film, tends to flourish in cycles and that these cycles usually occur during times of social stress. Carroll applies his theory to the twentieth century by giving examples from film history, for example German Expressionist horror films such as Friedrich Wilhelm Murnau's *Nosferatu* (1922) that emerged during the Weimar Republic, and the horror film cycle in the United States in the early 1950s during the early part of the Cold War (Carroll 1990, 207). Moreover, as Jeffrey Jerome Cohen suggests in his 1996 book, *Monster Theory: Reading Culture*, the monster in literature and film functions metaphorically as a cultural body, upon which we project our fears, anxieties, and taboos. In this sense the monster literally embodies cultural fears and anxieties (4).

In 1667, the early Enlightenment philosopher Samuel Pufendorf referred to the multitude of tiny principalities that constituted the Holy Roman Empire of the German Nation after the Thirty Years' War and the Peace of Westphalia as an "irregular body, similar to that of a monster" (n.p.).[1] This monster still haunted Germany in the eighteenth century and into the nineteenth century. Not until the Congress of Vienna in 1815 were the 314 territories that made up the Holy Roman Empire of the German Nation reduced to 39 (Fulbrook 2004, 101). Pufendorf's comment about the state of the Holy Roman Empire of the German Nation in the seventeenth century is an early use of the monster as a metaphor for social anxiety and stress, for example, during times of war. Less than one hundred years later, the monster poets used to address social anxieties and fears metaphorically would be the vampire—a logical choice at the time, considering the novelty and popular appeal that stories of central European vampires generated in western Europe. When German poets learned about the vampire of central European superstition from stories collected in Serbia and Hungary, they immediately adapted the new monster to address social anxieties, fears of death, and cultural taboos, much like Pufendorf had done in his analogy of Germany as an "irregular [monstrous] body."

During the first decades of the eighteenth century, poets, scientists, and philosophers in Germany and in other western European countries tried to come to terms with the vampire phenomenon that Austrian occupying forces in central Europe had relayed to the West. In 1716, the Ottoman Turks declared war on the Habsburgs after they had succeeded in driving the Venetians out of Peloponnesos and the Aegean archipelago and after the Habsburg Emperor Charles VI (1685–1740) had formed an alliance with the Venetians. The Turkish War was the final Habsburg victory for almost one hundred years. On August 5, 1716, the Habsburgs encountered the Ottoman army at Petrovaradin, Hungary, and defeated them under the command of Prince Eugene of Savoy, the Habsburgs' most esteemed commander and adviser. After this defeat of the Ottomans at Petrovaradin, Prince Eugene ultimately forced Belgrade to surrender, and he conquered northern Serbia. Meanwhile another Austrian army took Wallachia. On July 21, 1718, at Pozarevac (Passarowitz) in Serbia, peace was restored among Turkey, Austria, and Venice. As a result of the Peace of Passarowitz, the Habsburgs were able to keep their conquests in the Banat, eastern Slovenia, northern Serbia, and western Wallachia, and they were able to recover South Hungary. The Turks kept their conquests in Venice and Greece. Occupying forces from the Austrian armies remained in the areas acquired by the Habsburgs until 1739, and Charles VI commissioned them to record their observations of local customs and submit their reports to the court in Vienna. In his book *Vampires, Burial, and Death: Folklore and Reality*, cultural historian Paul Barber examines some of the reports in their cultural context and analyzes their broad societal impact. Among other more mundane observations, the occupying forces studied, reported, and officially recorded the peculiar local practice of exhuming bodies to prevent vampiric activity (Barber 2010, 5), a custom that understandably caught the attention of Western observers.

The emperor took great interest in the stories of vampiric activity and funded expeditions into these areas by doctors, clergy, scientists, and other officials, charging them with the task of documenting the alleged incidents of vampirism in his newly acquired territories and collecting stories of vampires from the corpus of local folklore. These reports mark the earliest documented sources of information on the central European vampire superstition that were available to poets in the West. Commanding officers stationed in Serbia repeatedly received orders from the emperor to investigate reports of vampirism in Serbian villages, and dutifully sent their reports back for review. The sheer quantity of correspondence between the court in Vienna and the officers stationed in Belgrade who were responsible for the investigation of vampirism and vampiric activity is itself quite remarkable. The growing interest in the stories of vampirism in Serbia was not, however, restricted to the court in Vienna; Charles VI circulated the reports among other ruling houses of the empire. A notably comprehensible and well-written account by an Austrian Army surgeon, Commander Johannes Flückinger,[2] played an important role in the increasing fascination with these superstitions throughout Europe (Bunson 1993, 99). Flückinger's report is variably entitled "Visum et Repertum" or "Arnod Paole," and tells the story of suspected vampirism in a Serbian village during the winter of 1731–1732. It caught the attention of many interested scientists and scholars in western Europe, including the ruling houses, which had received the previous reports from the emperor. These publications, in turn, attracted members of the literate middle and upper classes to what Barber refers to as "an early media event," in which educated Europeans encountered a very old superstition through relatively new media—articles in scientific journals, philosophical essays and treatises, and poems by popular poets (Bunson 1993, 5). These "public-relations representatives," inspired by Charles VI's investigations, transformed the vampire superstition of central Europe into a phenomenon that captivated the Enlightenment intelligentsia in the West. The reports and stories from the expeditions initially appeared in literary and political magazines published by the ruling house of Charles VI (Schroeder 1973, 37–69). Following these publications, essays on the vampire superstition originated at German universities and academies. This led to publications in scientific, political, social, and later even popular journals and magazines, which at this time were geared toward an ever-increasing reading public. By the mid-eighteenth century, the readership in most of Europe had expanded from being restricted to nobility and court society, as the authors themselves largely had been, to a growing educated middle class (Hoffmann and Rösch 1984, 90). In an effort to attract, retain, and entertain readers, journal editors were eager to publish the vampire stories. The first magazine to publish a report about the vampire superstition in Serbia was the *Wienerisches Diarium*. The article appeared in the July 21, 1725, issue of the magazine under the title "Copia eines Schreibens aus dem Gradisker Distrikt" (Copy of an Essay from the Gradisk District), identifying it as the story about a suspected vampire named Peter Plogojowitz that *Kameralprovisor* Frombald had written and submitted to court administrators in Vienna (Schroeder 1973, 41, 77). In fact, popular print media functioned as a direct link between the central European vampire stories and the first literary vampire when the first vampire poem was published in a scientific magazine in response to an article on the central European vampire stories. In 1748, Christlob Mylius, editor of the popular science magazine *Der Naturforscher* (The Natural Scientist), was planning to publish an article on the vampire stories from central Europe that had been collected for Charles VI. By publishing this article, Mylius was responding to the general fascination with the vampire superstition that had become popular by the middle of the century. It was his practice in his publication to follow each scientific article with a poem that reflected the article's theme, so he invited his friend, the German poet Heinrich August Ossenfelder, to write a poem that reflected the vampire theme. With the publication of his short poem, Ossenfelder barely escaped complete obscurity, and he is now recognized as the first poet to have adapted the vampire from folklore for creative literature.[3] What is unique and important about Mylius's scientific publication in 1748 is that it effectively marks the introduction of the vampire into literature through scientific inquiry and investigation by way of popular media.

Rationalists of the time explained that the alleged vampire epidemics were in reality the plague, or they sought other scientifically plausible explanations for this superstition.[4] The stories of Peter Plogojowitz, Arnod Paole, the vrykolakas, and the Romanian tale "The Vampire Princess" are examples of popular stories that reached Germany during this time (Schroeder 1973, 77). It is not surprising that the superstitions from central Europe were of particular interest to scientists, philosophers, and other scholars from the enlightened West, but the Enlightenment's pursuit of reason and its fight against superstition also made many people more aware of their mortality, preparing the way for the metaphorical signification of the vampire (Volckmann 1987, 156). Rational-thinking western European poets appropriated the "irrational" belief in vampires from central Europe in the form of a metaphor to address social ills. The vampire figure has been an important part of legends and mythologies on a global scale since mankind has told stories that express his fears of death, but at a time in the eighteenth century when it became important to explain such superstitions in a rational manner, the vampire found a new home as a metaphor in creative literature.

A close examination of the central European folklore that attracted German poets reveals different types of vampire tales and diverse images of the vampire figures that are at the root of the many traits we associate with the literary vampire today. The images of the vampire in the central European folklore that informed German poets vary somewhat depending on the country from which the folklore stems. The culturally based differences among the stories call attention to this monster's complexity, but also its malleable nature, a useful trait for storytelling purposes. The following folktales are the most popular representatives of a host of vampire stories from central Europe, southeastern Europe, and Greece that greatly influenced western European writers as they developed and constantly reinvented the literary vampire. The most popular reports of vampire stories collected for Charles VI that have survived are the Serbian folktale about Peter Plogojowitz from 1725; the story of the Greek, Vrykolakas, recorded by French botanist Pitton de Tournefort in 1702; "The Shoemaker from Silesia"; and the "Vampire Princess" from Romanian folklore. Of these, the stories of Peter Plogojowitz and "The Shoemaker of Silesia" were especially popular and influential in western Europe.

Most vampire folktales follow one of two common types. One is that a person from a village dies and is buried properly. Shortly thereafter family members and others die unexpectedly and inexplicably. The first to die becomes the scapegoat for the deaths following his. He is accused of returning to kill members of his family or community by sapping or draining their energy and leaving them pale or weak and apparently devoid of blood, to die shortly thereafter. Although the alleged incidents of "vampirism" were instead epidemics of illness in the community, the inexplicable nature of the illness, combined with the local superstitions, often led villagers to scapegoat the first to die. A second common type of tale is that of the future revenant, who dies violently, either by murder or suicide, and returns to haunt others in the community. Sometimes people die and the revenant is blamed for the haunting or the deaths. In many of the stories that belong to this tale type, the suspected vampire was not well liked when alive because he was of a generally malevolent nature. If the person who died violently and was disliked as a mortal was well known, then it seems natural that people might identify him as a monster and ascribe mischievous behavior in the community to his malicious behavior when alive. Common to stories from both tale types is that the townspeople exhume and examine the body of the accused revenant, noting in particular that the body appears fresh with evident growth of hair and nails, despite the fact that it had been buried for weeks or months. The body looked more alive than dead to the people who exhumed it because of their lack of knowledge of the decomposition process.[5] After making these key observations and after the presiding authorities had determined that the exhumed body was in fact a vampire, it became necessary to "kill" the revenant either by decapitation, staking, burning, or any combination of these, according to local belief and practice. Usually any unexplained deaths ceased after the revenant was destroyed.

An example of the first type of vampire tale involving a member of a community who died of a strange illness and returned after being buried is the Serbian tale of Peter Plogojowitz. As is typical for this tale type, vampirism occurs as an epidemic in a village and the first to die, Peter Plogojowitz in this case, is held responsible for the deaths that follow. Before they died, Plogojowitz's victims actually publicly accused him of coming to them while they were asleep and attempting to suffocate them. In accordance with the tale type, the body of the revenant was exhumed and found to be relatively fresh. According to Paul Barber, "it is generally assumed that the 'wild signs' [observed on Plogojowitz's corpse] imply that the corpse was believed to have an erection" (Barber 2010, 9). Barber goes on to explain that these "erections" result from the bloating of decomposition, an example of a symptom of decomposition that makes a body appear to be "alive" to the layman observer. This, the apparent growth of nails and hair, and moans or groans heard after staking are all symptoms of decomposition or sounds resulting from gas escaping from a decomposing body as a result of staking. The typical method of destroying the vampire by staking is especially common in Slavic folklore, such as this tale from Serbia.

The French King Louis XIV's (1638–1715) botanist, Pitton de Tournefort, was a member of an expedition charged with collecting specimens for the Sun King's gardens in 1700 when his travels took him to the Greek island of Mykonos, making him an unsuspecting witness to a supposed case of epidemic vampirism. He wrote his report about the vrykolakas in *A Voyage to Levant* (1702). *Vrykolakas* is the Greek term for a vampire or vampire-like creature and is an example of the second type of vampire tale, involving a person who was disliked as a mortal, died violently, and returned to wreak havoc on the community. In this image of the vampire, however, the monster is not blamed for any deaths. Instead, he causes mischief in the community. The story that Tournefort recorded focused on a peasant from the island of Mykonos who was disagreeable by nature, a point that Tournefort emphasizes as an important trait in this culture for his identity as a vampire after his death. The common characteristics of the Greek vrykolakas and the Slavic vampire are that the body of the revenant appears undecomposed, with no signs of rigor mortis when exhumed. In the case of the vrykolakas, however, the heart is removed and burned in order to "kill" it because, it is believed, a revenant cannot function without a heart. As a scientist from the enlightened West, it is not surprising that Tournefort takes a skeptical and dismissive tone when he reports about the peasants' superstitions and the manner in which they examined the suspected vampire's body:

> The butcher of the town, quite old and maladroit, began by opening the belly rather than the chest. He rummaged about for a long time in the entrails, without finding what he sought, and finally someone informed him that it was necessary to cut the diaphragm. The heart was torn out to the admiration of all the bystanders. But the body stank so terribly that incense had to be burned, but the smoke, mixed with the exhalations of this carrion, did nothing but increase the stench, and it began to inflame the minds of these poor people. . . . They took it into their heads to say that a thick smoke was coming from the

body, and we did not dare say that it was the incense. . . . After all our reasoning, they were of a mind to go to the seashore and burn the heart of the deceased, who in spite of this execution became less docile and made more noise than ever. (quoted in Barber 2010, 22)

Tournefort's final analysis after his experience with the vampire superstition in Mykonos is succinct: "the Greeks of today are not the great Greeks, and . . . there is among them only ignorance and superstition" (quoted in Barber 2010, 24). There is no mistaking Tournefort's disappointment in the superstitious tendencies of a society that had once produced some of the greatest thinkers in Western civilization.

"The Shoemaker from Silesia" is another example of the second type of vampire tale, in which the person who returns died before his time, either by murder, suicide, or an accident. The difference between this revenant and the Greek vrykolakas, however, is that the alleged vampire was not necessarily disliked when alive. In the Silesian story, a problem results from the attempt by the shoemaker's family to cover up the fact that he committed suicide, a disgrace that would have denied him a Christian burial. By claiming that he had died of a stroke, his wife was able to bury him "with great ceremony, in the manner of those who are pious and distinguished . . . as though he had led a holy and guilt-free life and had been a splendid Christian" (quoted in Barber 2010, 11). Suspicions by villagers that the man had in fact committed suicide and had not died of a stroke led to claims that he had returned to torment them physically, lying down on top of them in their beds and smothering them, as some vampires from Slavic folklore are wont to do when proper burial practices are disregarded. In this story, the revenant is portrayed as a ghost-like figure rather than as a walking corpse, but his alleged act of physically smothering his victims in their sleep connects him to the larger corpus of Slavic vampire folklore. Similarities with revenants from other central European tales, and the revenant's identity as a vampire, are particularly evident in the appearance of his body when exhumed. Again, it appears not to be dead and looks undecomposed. It is subsequently "killed" in a variety of ways: the body is decapitated, its hands and feet are dismembered, the back is cut open and the heart is removed, and it is finally burned on a funeral pyre. In this story, nothing is left to chance.

In his book *A Clutch of Vampires* (1974), the cultural historian Raymond McNally records vampire folktales ranging in origin from North America to China. One of the folktales, "The Vampire Princess," was preserved in the Institute of Folklore in Bucharest, Romania, and retrieved by McNally for his book. In this story, the young woman who dies and becomes a vampire is the daughter of an emperor. She dies from a broken heart because her father dismissed a soldier to whom she had taken a liking. Upon her death, the emperor has his daughter's tomb guarded by soldiers. Each night she rises from her tomb and eats the soldiers who are keeping watch. This continues until the emperor orders the woman's former lover to guard her tomb. On the advice of a beggar woman, the soldier hides in the church in three different places for three consecutive nights. He finally breaks the curse of the princess's existence as a vampire on the third night by hiding in her coffin once she has risen from it to find him. When she returns to her coffin, she sees him and becomes mortal again. Through his love and devotion to her and through his resourcefulness, the soldier breaks the curse, a common task for princes in fairy tales. This story is of particular interest here because it holds closely to the defined folklore tale type 307, "The Princess in the Shroud," from Antti Aarne's folklore index *The Types of the Folk-Tale: A Classification and Bibliography*. In his *Motif-Index of Folk-Literature* (1956), a translation and expansion of Aarne's book, folklorist Stith Thompson lists the individual motifs that occur in the Romanian tale, "The Vampire Princess": "E251 Vampire: A corpse that rises from the grave at night and sucks blood; D701 Gradual disenchantment; and N825.2 Old man helper." Here, however, the helper is the old beggar woman and the princess does more than just suck blood (Aarne 1971, 49). In contrast to Aarne's tale type 307, however, the soldiers who were killed are not resuscitated, and it is not stated definitively that the two marry and live happily ever after, although it might be assumed. This Romanian story differs from the others not only in its fairy-tale quality, but also in the fact that the vampire is a young woman. In most central European folklore, such as "Peter Plogojowitz" and the "Shoemaker of Silesia," the vampire is male and his appearance is only described superficially, if at all. The image of a woman as a vampire who is rescued from her cursed existence by her lover's kiss immediately eroticizes the folkloric vampire, who until now had been nothing more than a reanimated corpse.

The Romanian tale is also important because it reflects the common folkloric belief that people who die and leave something unresolved or a loved one behind will come back and wander restlessly, sometimes acting maliciously like a vampire or a ghost, until they are released from the curse. Many German poets adapted and modified this basic trait for their vampire poems and stories. The eroticization of the vampire as it is represented in the motif of the dead lover who returns marks the Romanian story as a nexus between the traditional folkloric vampire and its counterpart in creative literature. In the earliest vampire poems and stories by German poets, the erotic and seductive (often female) vampire was a standard feature. In contrast to later vampire fiction that focuses on a victim's lingering death for reasons of plot construction, as in Sheridan Le Fanu's novella, *Carmilla* (1872), and Bram Stoker's *Dracula* (1897), in folklore the purpose of the story is to identify a deceased person as a vampire in order to explain an epidemic or to show how bad behavior in life is punished upon death. In a fictional piece such as Le Fanu's, for example, a lengthy illness is an effective dramatic device that builds suspense. By emphasizing the duration of the illness, the intensity of the fear, the hallucinations, and the strangulations, Le Fanu successfully sets up the reader for the climax when the heroine, Laura, becomes afflicted with the very same illness that others before her had experienced before they succumbed to the vampire's attack. In folktales such as the ones mentioned here, however, it is only important to mention briefly how the alleged vampire lived and how he died, which explains why the death of the victim is often sudden and unexpected, as in the case of Peter Plogojowitz (Barber 2010, 7).

From this small sample of vampire tales it becomes evident that the causes of vampirism elaborated upon in central European folklore are as diverse as the methods employed for a vampire's destruction. Most often the vampire is male, and he has a zombie-like or ghost-like demeanor as a revenant. Although folkloric vampires may exhibit ghost-like qualities, however, they should not be confused with ghosts, which are disembodied spirits. Vampires appear in corporeal form to the humans they seek out, not as ethereal spirits. Usually, the vampire revenant from folklore does not suck blood or kill, and he returns to haunt his own community or relatives—not strangers. This image shows, then, that a vampire is not as easily defined as one might expect. In fact, one significant development of the literary vampire in the eighteenth century, which can be traced to its diverse portrayals in the folklore from central Europe, is that the vampire becomes as complex a creature as regular mortals are; it becomes a human-seeming monster with personality, passion, and purpose. Its monstrous nature, however, connects it metaphorically to the more sinister side of the human condition and the culture it lives in or invades. The vampire princess from the Romanian tale, for example, is a monster who evokes pity because she died leaving a loved one behind to break the curse of her damned existence. She is in this way a very human monster, a beautiful woman with feelings of longing, desire, and love, and yet she is also a merciless and cannibalistic killer. This is the ambiguous nature of the vampire that must have so intrigued western European poets that it was adopted immediately as a metaphor for the polarity of human nature and society. The other vampires from the Serbian, Greek, and Silesian tales are nothing more than mindless walking corpses or ghost-like figures, and the stories' narratives have a more typically folkloric, report-like quality than the more creative fairy-tale narrative quality of the Romanian folktale.

Once published, these stories inspired debate in western Europe among philosophers, poets, and scientists on the possibility of the actual existence of vampires. In 1728, the German theologian and academic Michael Ranft wrote what is still recognized today as one of the first and most thorough historical reports on vampirism in Europe, an essay bearing the rather colorful title "Über das Kauen und Schmatzen der Todten in Gräbern" (On the

Chewing and Smacking by the Dead in their Graves). In 1734, he published an expanded edition of his treatise. In keeping with the times, Ranft wrote his report in what he called a rationalist manner, in contrast to what he considered the emotional and enthusiastic styles of his contemporaries. While his colleagues' reports were intended to comply with enlightenment methodology, in Ranft's assessment they remained mostly unscientific. Ranft's report is more in compliance with the philosophy and methodology of the Enlightenment because he seeks answers to the vampire phenomenon in nature. In his report, Ranft explains that the apparent lack of decay in corpses identified as vampires results from the condition of certain types of soil and chemical processes in the soil, in which the bodies of the suspected vampires had been buried. Modern forensic science confirms Ranft's hypotheses of the effects of soil on the physical process of decay. Soil composition, climate, and the presence or absence of air, moisture, microorganisms, moderate temperatures, and insects are some of the important factors that affect decomposition rate, to which Ranft alludes in his essay (Barber 2010, 106–7).

Some of the philosophers and writers who took part in the debates sparked by the stories and wrote essays on the topic were the German theologian Christoph Friedrich Demelius, the French cleric and theologian Dom Augustin Calmet (1672–1757), and French philosophers and writers Voltaire (1694–1778) and Jean-Jacques Rousseau (1712–1778). Even the Royal Prussian Society of the Sciences compiled a report on vampirism based on observations made by medical doctors who traveled to central Europe for this purpose (Sturm and Völker 1968, 441–501). Demelius's essay, "Philosophischer Versuch, ob nicht die merckwürdige Begebenheit derer Blutsauger in Niederungarn, anno 1732 geschehen, aus denen principiis naturae erleutert werden" (A Philosophical Attempt to Determine Whether or Not the Strange Incident of Vampires in Lower Hungary in the Year 1732 Occurred, from Which Natural Principles Were Explained) is much like Ranft's in its attempt to explain the vampire superstition in a rationalistic manner. Calmet wrote several essays on the vampire phenomenon, most notably "Dissertations sur les apparitions des Esprits, et sur les vampires ou les revenans de Hongrie, de Moravie, etc." ("Dissertations upon the Apparitions of Angels, Daemons, and Ghosts, and Concerning Vampires of Hungary, Bohemia, Moravia and Silesia", 1746), which was translated into English in 1759. In 1751 he wrote two more treatises on vampires, "Traité sur les apparitions des esprits et sur les vampires ou les revenants de Hongrie, de Moravie &c" ("Treatise on the apparitions of ghosts and on the vampires or revenants from Hungary, Moravia, etc.") and "Dissertations sur les revenants en corps, les excommuniés, les oupires ou vampires, brucolaques, etc." ("Treatise on Vampires and Revenants: The Phantom World: Dissertation on Those Persons Who Return to Earth Bodily, the Excommunicated, the Oupires or Vampires, Vroucolacas, etc."). In his essays, Calmet systematically refutes the commonly observed characteristics of suspected vampires, such as the apparent postmortem growth of hair and nails, which he attributes to the continued circulation of bodily fluids after death (Sturm and Völker 1968, 480). Moreover, Calmet alludes to the problem of premature burial and explains that the typical screams and groans emitted by suspected vampires who were exhumed and subsequently staked occurred because they had been prematurely buried. This fear of being buried alive, sparked anew by the stories of vampirism and such rationalizations as Calmet's, brought about changes to burial practices, many of which have become commonplace.[6] Such premature burials occurred frequently enough that people made provisions in their wills for the interment of their bodies to be delayed, sometimes as long as three days.[7] Although he claims that the stories of vampires are so extraordinary that they do not even deserve any serious refutation, this is apparently Calmet's intent in writing his essay (Sturm and Völker 1968, 481). In it, Calmet calls for scientific proof and rational explanations of the vampire phenomenon rather than unchallenged and unquestioned belief in them. He does not, however, claim that there is no such thing as vampires, but rather that there simply is no proof of their existence. In an Age of Reason, however, his unwillingness to condemn vampirism outright as superstition, and his conclusion that there is simply no proof against their existence, struck a chord with rationalists at the time (Bartlett and Idriceanu 2008, 20).

Almost immediately after the first vampire stories from central Europe had begun to circulate throughout western Europe, the vampire was used as a political and social metaphor. For example, the English periodical, *The Gentleman's Magazine*, in May 1732 published a satirical article in response to the vampire story of Arnod Paole by Flückinger, treating the story of Paole as a metaphor for dreadful social conditions (Melton 1999, 481). A few decades later, Voltaire responded to the European vampire craze in his *Philosophical Dictionary* (1764) by using the vampire as a metaphor for economic exploitation in an essay on the pervasive interest learned men had in the vampire phenomenon. In it, he exclaims in disbelief:

> What! Vampires in our Eighteenth Century? Yes. . . . In Poland, Hungary, Silesia, Moravia, Austria and Lorraine—there was no talk of vampires in London, or even Paris. I admit that in these two cities there were speculators, tax officials and businessmen who sucked the blood of the people in broad daylight, but they were not dead (although they were corrupted enough). These true bloodsuckers did not live in cemeteries, they preferred beautiful places. . . . Kings are not, properly speaking, vampires. The true vampires are the churchmen who eat at the expense of both the king and the people. (quoted in Frayling 1991, 31)

In his satirical essay, Voltaire introduces the vampire as a metaphor for the predatory nature of clergy, businessmen, and even stock market traders in

Paris and London specifically, who suck the life from the common people but who are certainly not dead, just rotten to the core.

Scientists and philosophers continued their attempts to intellectually debate vampirism, some claiming that it was an actual disease, and others making the sociological observation that commoners told stories of vampire encounters while more highly educated people did not. Others were convinced that there was a rational explanation for the belief in vampirism. One correspondent in Berlin for the journal *Gazettes des Gazettes* was not satisfied with the rationalization of vampirism as mass hysteria put forth by philosophers. In an article published on November 1, 1765, he made the sarcastic claim that "[vampirism] is proved by so many facts that no one can reasonably doubt its validity, given the quality of the witnesses who have certified the authenticity of those facts" (quoted in Bartlett and Idriceanu 2008, 25). In his article, the correspondent challenges scientists to refute this evidence that had been recorded by eyewitnesses. Much like Voltaire in his use of the vampire as a political metaphor, Rousseau responded to the article in the *Gazettes des Gazettes* with social commentary and criticism of the legal system and the media:

> For some time now, the public news has been concerned with nothing but vampires; there has never been a fact more fully proved in law than their existence, yet despite this show me a single man of sense in Europe who believes in vampires or would even deign to take the trouble to check the falseness of the facts. (quoted in Frayling 1991, 32)

For Voltaire and Rousseau, the barrage of stories about vampirism and the fact that some of these were taken seriously as reliable eyewitness accounts was a testimony to the fickleness and gullibility of the populace. Despite the efforts by these philosophers and by scientists to explain away such superstitions, people in general remained captivated by the idea of the vampire. In fact, the apparent paradox of a fascination with vampires in an Age of Reason is actually a prime example of the spirit of the Enlightenment (Bartlett and Idriceanu 2008, 26). The birth of modern Freemasonry in the early eighteenth century, for example, ran parallel with advancements in science and enlightenment philosophical ideas, but it sparked an increasing attraction among the uninitiated to its rituals, secrecy, and mysteries, which resulted in a related interest among the people in all things occult. All the efforts by scientists and philosophers to fight superstition were not able to diminish human fascination with the supernatural.

On a related note, Charles VI's keen interest in the central European vampire superstition may explain his rather peculiar habit of exhuming his ancestors' remains and moving them to various locations in the empire. For more than four hundred years, the Habsburgs had been buried in Basel and in

Königsfelden. In 1739, Charles had the ancestral vault opened and requested an examination of the contents. He died in 1740, before any further investigation could be completed, and his eldest daughter, Maria Theresa (1717–1780), became the only woman ever to occupy the Habsburg throne. In 1770, she completed the task that her father had begun thirty years earlier and had the ancestral remains transported to a new vault in St. Blasien in the Black Forest. In 1807, Maria Theresa's grandson, Francis II, continued this practice of exhuming the bodies of ancestors and moving them to new locations that were under Habsburg rule.

By the time Maria Theresa became empress, enlightenment ideas had begun to permeate the empire, reaching Vienna from Germany and Italy. Toward the end of the eighteenth century, Vienna had become a center of enlightenment thought in its own right; the spirit of enlightenment thinking spread throughout the empire and into the Habsburgs' acquired lands in the Balkans. Though Maria Theresa generally disapproved of the doctrines of enlightenment philosophers, her policies as a ruler were deemed "rational, realistic, and practical" by her contemporaries (Mamatey 1987, 102). In the mid-eighteenth century, the persecution of witches in western Europe had begun to decline significantly, but was still widespread in Hungary and Poland. Already in 1682 Louis XIV had issued a royal decree, bringing an end to the legal persecution of witches in France, and in 1728 Friedrich Wilhelm I (1688–1740) followed suit. Maria Theresa, however, was inspired to put an end to witchcraft in her territories in response to stories of vampirism in these areas that continued to reach her court after her father's death, rather than as a result of the resurgence of witch-hunting in Hungary. After she had heard about the exhumation of a young woman's body in 1755 in the village of Hermersdorf, near the Silesian-Moravian border, and the subsequent disposal of the body as a vampire, Maria Theresa sent two of her court doctors to the village to investigate. After reading the report about this incident of suspected vampirism, she consulted with her primary court doctor, Gerard van Swieten, who advised her to ban this superstitious practice by legislative means as others before her had done when they addressed witchcraft in their territories. In March 1755, she issued a legal decree, forbidding these and other superstitions, such as magic and the persecution of witches. Less than one year later, in January 1756, she demanded that all the documentation on current witchcraft trials be submitted to her legal experts before the local courts could hand down any sentences. Maria Theresa's legal experts used modern scientific and legal arguments to attack the accusations made in the local courts and overturned most of the death sentences.

Charles VI's interest in stories of vampirism from his newly acquired territories in the Balkans, followed by his daughter's efforts to ban practices associated with this superstition and the persecution of witches in Hungary, resulted in a general association of Hungary with the vampire by western

Europeans (Klaniczay 1990, 179). Although central European vampire beliefs were essentially Greek and Slavic in origin, the most popular stories and reports that were circulating through Europe in the first half of the eighteenth century placed the vampire in Hungary and other neighboring countries, such as Romania. This connection between Hungary and the vampire becomes particularly apparent in the image of the vampire in the German poetry that introduced this monster into literature, most obviously when the poets name specific towns or geographic landmarks in these regions. The literary vampires in these early German poems and prose works also exhibit distinct characteristics that are primarily reminiscent of the vampires from the central European stories rather than Germany's own folklore, emphasizing their popular appeal at the time.

The literary vampire, then, was inspired by the vampire of superstition and folklore that western European officials, clergy, and scientists encountered through their observations in Hungary and Serbia during military occupation of the area. Despite the profound influence of the central European vampire stories, however, German poets were also able to draw on more familiar superstitions from German-speaking lands. German folklore and superstition does recognize vampire figures, but they differ greatly from the central European vampire stories in their basic traits and in the reasons for their existence. The German folkloric vampire tradition can be organized into three distinct categories: 1) the superstition of the *Nachzehrer*; 2) folksongs that center on the vampire as it connects with necrophilia; and 3) variations on the northern European Lenore legend.

The vampire figure from German superstition, known as the *Nachzehrer*,[8] is more of a disgusting nuisance than anything else (Bächtold-Stäubli and Hoffmann-Krayer 1942, 6:812). As its name implies, the *Nachzehrer* chews on itself and its shroud, but does not attack others. This type of superstition probably derives from the attempt to explain the disturbing state of bodies after grave robbery or after animals ate bodies that were buried in shallow graves. In volume 5 of the collection of German folksongs, *Deutsche Volkslieder mit ihren Melodien*, published by the German Folksong Archive in Freiburg, Germany, the editor Wilhelm Heiske distinguishes three types of folksongs with vampire themes that have in common a general theme of necrophilia associated with the female vampire and a happy ending between a man and his revenant bride: 1) "Der Färber" (The Dyer); 2) "Richmudis von Adocht"; and 3) "Die scheintote Braut" (The Seemingly Dead Bride) (Heiske and Seemann 1967, 235). Though several variations of each type of song have been collected, it will suffice here to summarize the basic plots in order to show the distinctions among the songs, as well as their similarities.

In the folksong type "Der Färber," a dyer asks for a young woman's hand in marriage, to whom he has already pledged his love, but he is rejected by her parents. He goes on his journeyman travels, but leaves behind a gold coin with the girl as a deposit toward their marriage. While he is away, the parents marry the girl to a wealthy widower. She becomes ill from a broken heart and dies. Soon afterward she appears to her lover, the dyer, as a ghost and he hurries back to the village. He is too late, because she has already been buried. That night he opens her grave and she rises from her coffin. He returns with her to her widower's home and this man faints. After six months the two lovers are married in a church (Heiske and Seemann 1967, 235). In the folksong type "Richmudis von Adocht," the woman, Richmudis von Adocht, dies and is placed in her coffin. According to her husband's wishes, her wedding band remains on her finger. That night the sexton and his assistant open Richmudis's coffin in order to steal her ring and are horrified to see that she is still alive. They flee the crypt and leave behind their lamp. Richmudis takes the lamp and goes to her husband's house. She calls to her husband to open the door for her. When a servant girl hears her, she runs to the husband to tell him. He opens the door for his wife who tells him that an angel from heaven awakened her. He is happy to see that she has returned from the dead and they share a meal together. She lives for seven more years, during which time she bears him seven sons (Heiske and Seemann 1967, 239). In the folksong type "Die scheintote Braut," two friends have children, one a son and one a daughter, who grow up together as very close friends. They promise each other that they will always be together, but one day a wealthy officer asks the girl's father for his daughter's hand in marriage. The father accepts and the girl must marry the officer instead of her beloved friend. At the wedding ceremony in the church, the bride collapses at the sight of her beloved and dies. The officer buries her in her wedding gown and wedding band. That night, the grave digger opens her grave in order to steal her wedding gown. When he turns her body to do this, she awakens and the grave digger flees in horror. She goes to her beloved friend's house and asks for clothing. He lets her into his house and keeps her hidden with him for one year. Since the grave digger had covered up the grave again, thinking her body was still in it, her secret is safe. When the officer finally dies at war, the couple reveals the secret of her return from the dead to their parents. Everybody is overjoyed and they marry. This is apparently the origin of the German saying, *Was Gott zusammenfügt, das bleibt und wird gebrochen nicht* (What God joins together, stays intact and will not be broken) (Heiske and Seemann 1967, 245). Clearly these folksongs are very similar to fairy tales, most obviously so in the use of the number seven in "Richmudis von Adocht," the happy ending, and the ability of true love to break a curse. Though the stories vary from one to the other in their basic plots, especially in the manner by which the woman rises from the dead—by the actions of her lover exhuming her ("Der Färber") or of her own accord because her grave is robbed ("Richmudis von Adocht" and "Die scheintote Braut")—they share a common feature: everyone lives happily ever after. Death cannot destroy a love that is meant to be and, in a manner reminiscent of fairy tales, the necrophilic undertones of the folksongs are not connected with an atmosphere of horror or death as a punishment, as they are in the later vampire poems and prose works by German poets.

The northern European Lenore legend represents a very different motif of the dead lover returning, and it is related to a motif listed in Antti Aarne's tale type index. In his classification of folktales, Aarne calls this particular motif, "The Dead Bridegroom Carries off his Bride." Coincidentally, he adds the subtext "Lenore" to the title of the motif. The description and title that Aarne provides for this motif are based on information he gathered from the *Child English and Scottish Popular Ballads* and from M. Böhm's article in the *Hessische Blätter für Volkskunde XVII* (1918) entitled "Der Lenorenstoff in der lettischen Volksüberlieferung" (The Lenore Material in Latvian Folklore). Aarne describes the motif, "The Dead Bridegroom Carries off his Bride," as follows: "He carries her behind him on his horse. Says, 'The moon shines bright, the dead ride fast,' etc. She is pulled into the grave" (quoted in Thompson 1956, 61). Aarne listed this motif under the division "Ordinary Folktales" and the subdivision "Tales of Magic—Supernatural Adversaries" in his index. Two other vampire tale types are listed as well: Number 307, "Princess in the Shroud," which applies to the Romanian folktale referred to earlier in this chapter; and number 363, "The Vampire," a variation of number 307. It is worth noting that the tale type "The Dead Bridegroom Carries off his Bride (Lenore)" is listed as number 365 and immediately follows 363. Aarne purposefully left numbers out in the middle of tale groups, such as this one, because his index was incomplete and he expected to add related tale types to certain groups of tales. This implies that tale type 365 belongs to a vampire group of tales and supports the argument that the Lenore legend has a vampire theme and not a ghost theme. Gottfried August Bürger adopted this motif for his poem "Lenore," with Wilhelm as the vampire. In his ballad "Die Braut von Korinth," Goethe reverses this motif when he has his female vampire return to her betrothed with the purpose of transforming their bridal bed into his death bed. The common theme among the many variations of the folksong type "Lenore" is that the dead lover returns from the grave to his wife or lover as a result of her excessive grief over his death. Typically, the woman dies by falling into the dead lover's grave, but in a more Christianized version of the "Lenore" folksong, "Das Lenorenmotiv im Schönhengster Land" (The Lenore Motif in the Land of Schönhengst), she dies and goes to heaven wearing a crown of flowers as a testament to her love and fidelity after the death of her lover.

The central European vampire from folklore and superstition varies greatly from the vampire in German folklore and superstition in the reasons for its existence as a revenant, and the effect it has on the living once it has risen from its grave. In the central European tradition, it is important to know how one can become a vampire (by violent death or suicide), and the vampire typically wreaks havoc or even kills people in its community. There are also numerous ways to put a vampire to its final death. In the German tradition, however, a person becomes a vampire because the body is exhumed ("Der Färber," "Richmudis von Adocht," and "Die scheintote Braut") or because of excessive mourning for a deceased lover ("Lenore"). Furthermore, it is common for the revenant and his or her mortal lover to live happily ever after, or as in the "Lenore" legend, she dies. As we will see in the following chapters, German poets were primarily influenced by the stories of vampirism from central Europe, though elements of cannibalism and necrophilia in the prose works in particular suggest a connection to the German superstition of the *Nachzehrer* and the folksongs.

Our modern perception of the vampire has been formed much like a mosaic, from an accumulation of images and metaphoric uses that have been passed down first through regional folklore and then from poet to poet and from artist to artist. The most famous vampire of fiction, Dracula, has been formed and greatly influenced by false associations with a historical Dracula. There is evidence in Bram Stoker's notes for his novel that he borrowed the name "Dracula" for his vampire from a historical "Voivode Dracula," which Stoker discovered during his research at Whitby Library. There is no evidence that Stoker was, in fact, referring to the historical Romanian Prince Dracula, also known as Vlad Tepes or Vlad the Impaler from Wallachia (1431–1476),[9] notorious for his habit of impaling his enemies' bodies in an effort to deter further aggressors.[10] This has been a common misperception that very likely stems from confusing the names of the Voivode Dracula with Prince Dracula (Vlad Tepes). The only documented connection between Stoker's Dracula and a historical Voivode Dracula is in Stoker's use of the name, very likely because it means the devil, a more appropriate and creative choice of a name than Stoker's original name for his vampire: Count Wampyre (Miller 2000, 187–88). Hence, the most famous literary vampire, Dracula, though localized in central Europe, does not have its origins in the vampire folklore of the Balkans as do the original vampires from the earliest German poems, but rather in the name of a historical figure from this region who had nothing to do with vampirism. While Stoker simply borrowed the name Dracula from a figure from Romanian history that had never been associated with the vampire until he used his name for his novel, there is a more direct link between the vampire of central European folklore and the German literary vampire. This link is evident in the first vampire poem by Ossenfelder.

It has been the purpose here to lay the groundwork for establishing a link between the vampire of central European folklore and superstition and the vampire of literature. In effect, the folkloric vampire became accessible to western European poets via the results of military conflict and the observations of military personnel stationed in the occupied territories of Hungary and Serbia upon the Habsburgs' conquest of these territories. The cultural link between the vampire of folklore and the literary vampire, then, was political upheaval, war, and western European occupation in a region where the vampire was not mere superstition, but a way of life, corresponding to the theories put forth by Noël Carroll and Jeffrey Jerome Cohen that horror stories flourish in times of social stress and that the monster functions as a cultural body for society's fears and anxieties. Scientific inquiry and popular fascination with this new monster led to cultural awareness of the central European vampire superstition in the West and the subsequent integration of this culture into western Europe via scientific articles, reports, and finally, literature. The literary link between the folkloric vampire and the literary vampire, provided by Ossenfelder in his poem, took place quite suitably in a popular scientific journal. Moreover, the widespread interest in the vampire that resulted in its use as a literary figure in the last half of the eighteenth century was not based on the idea of merely adapting regional superstition for a more creative literary medium. Instead, it was based on the distinctly Enlightenment scientific investigation of a superstition that led to scientific inquiries into death and the decomposition of bodies, and subsequently sparked discussion about the willingness of people to believe such superstitions in an Age of Reason. In fact, the scientific inquiry into the central European vampire phenomenon that was spearheaded by Charles VI was of an anthropological nature, especially if we remember that Charles VI initially charged occupying forces with the task of observing and recording the practices of the people in the lands he had won from the Ottoman Turks. It was only a matter of time before this fascinating superstition became increasingly accessible to the western European public in the poetry and prose written by eighteenth and nineteenth century poets, first in Germany and soon after in Britain and France.

NOTES

1. My translation of part of Pufendorf's statement: "Es bleibt uns also nichts anderes übrig, als das deutsche Reich . . . einen irregulären und einem Monstrum ähnlichen Körper zu nennen."

2. In an introductory statement to his translation of Flückinger's report, Barber mentions that several translations of this report exist and that several versions of the author's name exist for this reason, for example, "Fluchinger." Barber's translation is from a text published in Nuremberg in 1732 and reprinted in Dieter Sturm's and Klaus Völker's anthology, *Von denen Vampiren*.

3. This poem will be discussed in more detail in chapter 2.

4. At the time of numerous vampire reports from southeastern Europe in the eighteenth century there were also outbreaks of the plague. In 1710, for example, a vampire outbreak in East Prussia occurred simultaneously with a plague outbreak (Melton 1999, 211).

5. The apparent posthumous growth of hair and nails, which is in fact "a shedding of the nails, and loosening of the hair," is particularly noticeable, but is simply part of the natural

decomposition process (Barber 2010, 106). The "fresh" appearance of the corpse is attributable to a phenomenon known as "skin slippage," the "sloughing away" of the upper skin layer to reveal skin that is not actually new, but rather "raw-looking" (109).

6. Other burial rites that developed out of a fear of premature burial include the *conclamatio*, or thrice-repeated loud call of the allegedly deceased's name, the practice of adorning the body of the deceased, the practice of exposing the deceased's face, and the practice of waiting several days before burial or cremation (Ariès 1995, 506). Toward the end of the eighteenth century certain rooms were developed in which to deposit the allegedly deceased (*lieux de dépôt*), and the first funeral homes were actually called *vitae dubiae azilia*, or asylums of questionable life. From 1791 until 1818 such funeral homes were built in the German cities of Weimar, Berlin, Mainz, and Munich (511).

7. The oldest such will that Ariès was able to find dates back to 1662. He quotes from several of these wills through the late eighteenth century (Ariés 1995, 508–9). By the end of the nineteenth century, however, stories of premature burials had become less frequent, and doctors had begun increasingly to refute the possibility of any gray area between life and death. They maintained that there was either life or death, but nothing in between (513).

8. *Nachzehrer*: from the German *nach* (after) and *zehren* (to feed on).

9. To be more specific, Prince Dracula was born in Transylvania, in a fortified German town called Schassburg, or Sighisoara in Romanian (McNally and Florescu 1994, 15).

10. Though Dracula made wide use of impalement, it was not his innovation. Impalement was well known in Asia and was practiced in Turkey during the Middle Ages (McNally and Florescu 1994, 91).

Chapter Two

The First Vampire Poems

Since its inception into literature by German poets in the eighteenth century, the vampire has been one of the most popular monsters in literature and film, and German poets and filmmakers have been particularly innovative in their representation of this horror figure. The popular culture surrounding the vampire had already begun before mid-century after the reports of vampirism in central Europe spread westward. In 1748 Heinrich August Ossenfelder (1725–1801) published the first poem that featured a vampire, "Der Vampir" (The Vampire), and popular German poets such as Gottfried August Bürger (1747–1792) and Johann Wolfgang von Goethe (1749–1832) followed suit with two poems, "Lenore" in 1774 and "The Bride of Corinth" in 1797, respectively. Goethe's poem, "The Bride of Corinth," introduced the female vampire into literature; the poem was even more influential on an international scale than the first poems by Ossenfelder and Bürger, because by this time Goethe had already emerged as the leading poet and literary authority on the continent and, thus, his attention to this theme of the vampire in poetry legitimized its use for other poets (Melton 1999, 255). One year later, in 1798, Samuel Taylor Coleridge published his poem, "Christabel," which featured the first female vampire in English poetry. When Joseph von Eichendorff (1788–1857) published his vampire poems, "Das kalte Liebchen" (The Cold Sweetheart; 1816) and "Die spate Hochzeit" (The Late Wedding, 1828), the literary vampire had already achieved international recognition, especially in Britain and France.

    The vampire made its first mark in literature in ballad poetry in the mid-eighteenth century. In their vampire poetry, German poets introduced some of the most common and powerful motifs that are associated with the literary vampire and the cinematic vampire to this day.

Beginning with the first known vampire poem, "The Vampire" by Heinrich August Ossenfelder, the combination of the more common themes of "love" and "lover" with the vampire theme resulted in the creation of a new motif that has become fundamental to the literary vampire and more recently, the cinematic vampire, namely "dead lover returns." In the poems addressed here, the term *femme fatale*, which immediately conjures images of a beautiful and seductive yet destructive woman, becomes intensified in conjunction with the vampire theme, evident in the modern alternative term, "vamp." This newly intensified image of the vampire *femme fatale* reveals this figure's function in the plot of the narrative: she will seduce and kill a man, who is very likely also her lover, in good vampire fashion. Both Frenzel (1988, ix) and Lüthi (1980, 11) agree that motifs recur in narratives because they have entered collective human activity and thought through repeated applications and easy association with the plot of the narrative. Besides the universal occurrence of vampires or vampire-like figures in mythologies and folklore throughout Europe and Asia, by the mid-eighteenth century when the first vampire poem was written, the vampire had already established itself as part of a poet's "natural environment." Not long after Charles VI circulated throughout western Europe the vampire stories that he had collected from his occupied territories in central Europe, the curious phenomenon of the vampire became very much a part of the "natural environment" in western Europe, providing the themes and motifs that poets use for their work. As we have seen, the vampire was discussed at great length in universities, among scientists and medical doctors, articles were published in journals, and treatises were written and argued. The popular appeal and omnipresence of the vampire stories and intellectual debates on this phenomenon resulted in collective associations with the vampire, which facilitated an immediate use of motifs such as "dead lover returns" by the first poets. After all, the central European stories that the reading public had become familiar with centered on deceased loved ones who returned to haunt or kill people in their immediate families or communities. In the case of the story, "The Vampire Princess," the vampire's intended victim is her lover. Hence the vampire quickly became a theme of scholarly debate, a theme in literature and, later, a literary motif in the guise of "dead lover returns" and *femme fatale*.

Contemporary political and social problems or issues necessarily affect the prevalence of certain literary themes and motifs in poetic works. These social issues, which often reflect specific fears and anxieties such as war and the loss of loved ones to the ravages of war, infidelity, religious anxieties, and the curiosity and fear resulting from the stories of vampires flooding western Europe during the eighteenth century, became popular themes for poets. The application of popular themes in conjunction with varying motifs contributes to the sustainability of the theme over time (Frenzel 1966, 28). Contemporary social issues, philosophical trends, and scientific discoveries determine not only the prevalence of general literary themes, but also the predominance of certain motifs (Frenzel 1966, 72). The emergence and popularity of the vampire theme in German literature during the eighteenth century, especially in the horror poetry discussed here, are clearly influenced by social, political, scientific, and even philosophical concerns regarding the battle against superstition during the Enlightenment and the simultaneous confrontation with the vampire phenomenon from central Europe. Considering the frenzy of fascination that the vampire stories from central Europe caused in the enlightened West, it is no great wonder that the vampire found its way into western European literature soon after the stories had been circulated.

HEINRICH AUGUST OSSENFELDER: "DER VAMPIR" ("THE VAMPIRE")

When Christlob Mylius asked his friend Heinrich August Ossenfelder to write a poem for his scientific journal *Der Naturforscher* (The Natural Scientist), he gave him a specific topic to write about. In accordance with his concept for the journal, Mylius asked Ossenfelder to write a poem that reflected the theme of the article or story that preceded it in the publication. This particular item was the 125th letter from King Frederick the Great's friend, Boyer d'Argens, titled "Lettres juives," which Mylius published in two installments on May 18 and May 25, 1748. Boyer d'Argens' 125th letter is addressed to his friend Isaac, and in it he tells his friend about stories of vampires that he read in the journal, *Mercure Historique & Politique* (October 1736, 403–11). In his letter, d'Argens quotes the stories directly from his source and comments on them. One of these stories is "Visum et repertum (Arnod Paole)," written by Commander Johannes Flückinger for Emperor Charles VI.[1] Ossenfelder's vampire-themed poem bore the simple and straightforward title, "Der Vampir" ("The Vampire"), and represented the content of d'Argens's letter about the central European vampire superstition, specifically the story "Visum et repertum," in some detail. More importantly, Ossenfelder took this information from the vampire stories in d'Argens' letter and added new elements to the image of the vampire that would become canonical; in his short poem, Ossenfelder eroticized death and fear.

Today Ossenfelder is best known for the poem he published in this journal, and he goes down in history as the first poet to introduce the vampire into creative literature with his poem (Bunson 1993, 193; Melton 1999, 470). Aside from some negative reviews of his work by Erich Schmidt in volume 24 of the *Allgemeine Deutsche Biographie* (General German Biography, 1887), a compilation of biographical information on German poets, a brief mention by Karl Goedeke in his *Grundrisz zur Geschichte der deutschen*

Dichtung (Outline of the History of German Literature, 1989; vol. 3, 372–73 and vol. 4, 59–60) and by Stefan Hock in his book, *Die Vampyrsagen und ihre Verwertung in der deutschen Literatur* (The Vampire Legends and their Application in German Literature, 1900), Ossenfelder has received very little critical attention. In his biographical entry for Ossenfelder, Schmidt refers to the journal *Der Naturforscher* as a "physikalische Wochenschrift" (a "scientific weekly") (Schmidt 1887, 498). Goedeke also mentions Ossenfelder's regular contributions to Mylius's journal, but rather than discussing or even listing Ossenfelder's works, Goedeke is content to emphasize the fact that Lessing thought little of Ossenfelder's work (Goedeke 1989, vol. 4, 59). Although this short poem by Ossenfelder has only received marginal scholarly attention, it is very important for several reasons. In reference to Ossenfelder, Melton goes as far as to state: "The emergence of the modern literary vampire began with the exploration of the vampiric theme in German poetry" (Melton 1999, 470). In addition, Ossenfelder's poem addresses the eighteenth-century struggle to come to terms with superstition in an Age of Enlightenment by presenting the vampire as a metaphor for the threat that superstition posed to people and their religious faith. By presenting this theme in an anacreontic poem,[2] the threat to Christianity is likened to seduction. Ossenfelder's use of the vampire figure in the poem has the added effect of presenting this seduction as an act of aggression. Since the vampire figure generally represents death and destruction, rather than love, wine, friendship, and the enjoyment of life that are common themes in anacreontic poetry, the use of this figure by Ossenfelder in the style of anacreontic poetry is ironic at best.

Furthermore, and maybe even most significantly, Ossenfelder's poem establishes a direct and specific geographic link to northeastern Hungary as a source for the literary vampire, thus connecting it closely to the article on the vampire stories from central Europe that preceded it in the journal. Ossenfelder's poem begins with a first-person narrative introduction by the male vampire. It is apparent from the tone in the poem's first seven lines that the vampire is frustrated by the fact that his "dear young maiden" stubbornly believes in the Christian teachings of her devoutly religious mother, just as the people along the river Theyse believe in vampires (1.1–1.7):

> My dear young maiden clingeth
> Unbending, fast and firm
> To all the long-held teachings
> Of an ever-faithful mother;
> As folk along the Theyse
> Heyduck-like do believe
> In vampires that bring death.

The "Theyse" is the river Tisza, the longest river in Hungary, which originates in Ukraine and flows approximately 600 kilometers south from northeastern Hungary, near the border to Slovakia and Ukraine, to join the Danube in Serbia and Montenegro. In lines 10–12 of this poem, the vampire figure announces his precise geographic location along the Tisza when he says: "I will myself avenge / And today in Tockay / Drink thee to a vampire."[3] Tockay is the German name for a town situated along the western bank of the river Tisza in northeastern Hungary between the larger cities of Miskolc to the west and Nyíregyháza to the east.

The precise geographic location given in this poem is important because it associates the first known literary vampire with an area of central Europe where the stories of vampirism collected for Emperor Charles VI originated. Commander Flückinger's report, "Visum et Repertum,"[4] is a response to investigations of vampirism in Serbia, specifically east of the "Tisa,"[5] close to the Transylvanian Alps in Romania. The setting of Ossenfelder's poem along the Tisza and its purpose in Mylius's journal as a poetic representation of the vampire stories is indisputable proof that the modern European literary vampire was influenced by the stories of vampirism that were collected for Charles VI in Hungary, Serbia, and Romania. It may also have been important for Ossenfelder to provide a precise setting for his poem because he was aware that the readership of his friend's journal would immediately associate these areas in Hungary with the vampire stories that had been circulating throughout western Europe and had captivated the interest of so many people, and because the readership was very likely familiar with Flückinger's popular scientific report.

By accusing the young woman in this poem of stubbornly believing in the moral precepts put forth by her mother, just as the simple people along the Tisza believe "heyduck-like" in vampires,[6] the vampire equates her strict old-fashioned beliefs, taught by Christianity, with the superstition of vampires. Christianity to him is just another superstitious belief, and his tone implies that her faith angers him. This reaction to her faith brings to the forefront the superstition-religion dialectic that prevailed during the Enlightenment. The vampire phenomenon in central Europe was investigated by Western scientists, who were thus able to develop theories about decomposition and the determination of the moment of death. Hence, the vampire phenomenon as it was investigated in the eighteenth century was initially a scientific phenomenon, which in turn explains why debates on this subject were conducted at universities and why the first poem with a vampire theme was published in a scientific journal. Ossenfelder's poem, then, thematizes the divide between religion and science that grew out of the Enlightenment struggle against superstition. In fact, one might go so far as to say that the vampire in Ossenfelder's poem represents scientific superstition while the young woman, his intended victim, represents religious superstition.

The Enlightenment was also the epoch during which the German bourgeoisie made great strides in developing its self-assertion as a social class and related efforts to define itself in comparison to the aristocracy. Instead of defining itself merely according to its position in the social hierarchy, the bourgeoisie defined itself according to moral standards that set it apart from the perceived lack of morals in the aristocracy. For example, the bourgeoisie put a strong emphasis on cultivating certain values that had the purpose of defining it as a group. These values included morality, virtue, and dignity in all things. In the German literature of this period, aristocratic corruption of bourgeois innocence is a particularly common theme (Kaiser 1976, 53; Stollberg-Rilinger 2000, 86, 93). Ossenfelder's poem reflects this bourgeois struggle against the corruption of morality, though it is not clear that the vampire figure is necessarily a member of the aristocracy. Regardless, the fact that the intended lover in this poem appears as a vampire signifies that he will cause death and destruction. The fact that he promises to seduce the young woman indicates that he will at the very least destroy her virtue, bringing about the death of a part of her identity that is defining and crucial and of greater metaphoric significance than the corruption of a mere individual. This is especially evident when one considers that she is identified in this poem only by her religious faith.

The poem is addressed directly to the young woman whose name is Christiane,[7] very likely derived from the Latin *christianae*, meaning "of a Christian" and stemming from *christianitas*, the Latin word for Christianity. In fact, the young woman is the daughter of a very devout Christian mother, hence she is literally "of a Christian." The vampire's use of the German diminutive form of her name, Christianchen, is the reader's first clue that he has an emotional connection to her. It is likely that he is (or was) a suitor whose love for her was not reciprocated or acknowledged because of her strong religious faith. This becomes particularly apparent in the next several lines of his direct address to her when he expresses his plan to take her by force if she will not reciprocate his affections (1.8–1.12):

> But my dear Christiana, just wait,
> Thou dost not want to love me;
> I will myself avenge
> And today in Tockay
> Drink thee to a vampire.

For the remainder of the poem he explains to her how she will feel when he has completed his seduction of her. The images that Ossenfelder uses in the vampire figure's explanation of how he will seduce her imply that he will rape her since she is unwilling to consent (1.13–1.21):

> And as softly thou art sleeping
> From thy lovely cheeks
> Will suck fresh crimson color
> And so shalt thou be startled
> When I kiss thee thus

The First Vampire Poems 27

> And as a vampire kiss:
> When then thou dost truly tremble
> And limply in my arms
> Dost sink like one dead.

In the context of his sexually aggressive seduction of her in these lines, her trembling and the image that she will sink into his arms like a dead person would seem to imply that he expects that he will in fact bring her to orgasm—an additional insult, considering his aggressive intentions. After he explains what he will do to her sexually, he asks if his teachings are better than her mother's.

Her mother's teachings are the teachings of Christianity. But what are his teachings? On the one hand, as a vampire from northeastern Hungary, he embodies the superstitions told by the people in the area of northern Hungary near the town of Tokay, with which he is apparently very familiar. In his embodiment of the superstitions of central Europe, the vampire figure in this poem becomes a representative of central European superstition in general, which is in turn associated with an area of the world that was considered backward and even dangerous to western Europeans at this time in history. On the other hand, as a vampire, he is necessarily destructive and associated with death. As a revenant who plans to attack his victim in a sexual manner, he also represents the universal taboo of necrophilia, which functions here as a physical manifestation of the common warning in folklore against excessive love or even lust for the dead that will not allow the dead to rest. The vampire aggressor in this poem represents the hostile threat posed by superstition in the struggle between the superstitious beliefs of the people of Hungary and of Christianity. In this poem then, superstition is a male aggressor, namely a vampire, the monstrous Other associated with central Europe, who has the malicious intent to destroy or corrupt his victim, Christianity, through seduction and the draining of its life force, represented by blood. The added element provided by the anacreontic context of this poem functions specifically to juxtapose the strict moral values of society, represented by the religious values of the mother and daughter, with the possibility of a destructively hedonistic lifestyle, represented by the vampire figure's planned seduction.

As the male vampire in this poem describes it, there will be no effective resistance from his victim when he attacks, though this should not be understood as consent on her part. Holding true to his guise as a vampire based in central European folklore, he plans to attack while his victim sleeps: "And as softly thou art sleeping / From thy lovely cheeks / Will suck fresh crimson color" (l.13–1.15). His teachings are that superstition poses the greatest threat to Christianity when Christianity "sleeps" or is not conscious of any threats. Hence, superstition is able to seduce and corrupt Christians if they are not aware of the threat or if they are complacent. In the image of the vampire from Hungary, superstition takes on a destructive quality that threatens the morals of the enlightened western European from the outside. The threat is made by a figure that is foreign to the enlightened West, but was brought to the West by cultural interaction between western Europe and central Europe. The message expressed in this poem is intended for the enlightened reader and warns against the danger posed by superstition, which is associated with central Europe, and which has the power to destroy if it is underestimated or if it goes unheeded.

In his poem, Ossenfelder combines common vampire traits from the reports, such as the attack by a male vampire while the victim sleeps and the geographic location, with new traits that came to define vampires in later literary works. Ossenfelder's innovations concerning the characteristics of the vampire figure in this poem are fourfold: 1) the story is told from the vampire's perspective; 2) the vampire's victim will become a vampire herself—"I will myself avenge / And today in Tockay / Drink thee to a vampire" (l.10–1.12); 3) there is an erotic element involved in the encounter between the vampire and his victim—"When I kiss thee thus / And as a vampire kiss" (l.17–1.18) which represents rape in the context of this poem; 4) Christianity as an institution is the vampire's enemy; in folklore, Christian symbols such as the cross were used to repel potential vampire attacks, simply because they were understood to be effective against evil in general.

In Ossenfelder's poem, the vampire promises to come to "Christianchen" in her sleep. By clearly stating that he will visit his beloved in her sleep, Ossenfelder's vampire—whether real or projected—demonstrates a close connection to the vampire of superstition and folklore. The presence of the vampire in the dream of his victim has no other function in this poem because it is the vampire himself who announces what he will do. These early literary vampires' habits of approaching their victims as they sleep is not surprising when one remembers that the vampires from folklore were inclined to torment their victims as they slept. The point in which this poem differs in its narrative from the original folklore and reports, however, is that the point of view in the poem is that of the vampire. As a representative of old-world superstition, the vampire in this poem is in control. He says exactly what he will do to his victim and when he will attack. He will suck her blood, and he will do this as she sleeps. In contrast to the later poems by Bürger and Goethe, the dream motif is nothing more than a "fact" borrowed from the folklore that indicates the time when the vampire will attack.

The irony in this poem is evident in the appearance of a vampire figure in an anacreontic poem. Considering the life-affirming themes that prevail in this genre of poetry, such as wine, love, and merriment, the vampire seems out of place (Best 1987, 119). Ossenfelder's connection of such a carefree genre of poetry with the vampire theme is essentially a perversion of the genre. In fact, the only anacreontic elements in the poem are eroticism and the passing reference to wine with the word "Tockay," but this is nevertheless enough to identify it as anacreontic poetry. Through his use of the vampire as the seducer in this poem, Ossenfelder adds a sinister quality to the otherwise cheerful hedonistic atmosphere that is typical of this style of poetry. In so doing, he introduces the image of the vampire as a figure who is simultaneously erotic and dangerous; he is the seducer unto a hedonistic lifestyle—an image that would prevail into present times. As an anacreontic poem, "Der Vampir" treats the vampire as an aggressive seducer of the virtuous, the instigator and proponent of a destructive hedonistic existence, to which it is easy to succumb. It would be only a matter of time before this fascinating subject matter became increasingly accessible to the western European public in the ballads written by later eighteenth-century German poets, such as Bürger and Goethe, and in the poetry, stories, and novels produced by German and British poets during the nineteenth century.

GOTTFRIED AUGUST BÜRGER: "LENORE" ("LENORA")

Gottfried August Bürger was an admirable publicist with regard to his own work, specifically his poem, "Lenore." Even before he began working on the ballad and then during the months he spent working on it, he was in constant contact with friends from the "Göttinger Hainbund," who made suggestions for improvement and encouraged him. Bürger was very confident of his ballad's success, and was even advised by his friends to be more modest in his publicity of it (Schmidt-Kaspar 1986, 229). Even before the ballad went to print, copies of "Lenore" were in circulation throughout Germany. "Lenore" aroused great approval, disapproval, and also accusations of blasphemy. As a result of its publication of "Lenore," the *Göttinger Musenalmanach* was banned in Vienna—the capital of an Austria whose regime enjoyed close ties to the Catholic Church. Yet even Bürger's inflated confidence seems modest compared to the ballad's sensational national and international success, and the enduring place it has held in German literature ever since as one of the first *Kunstballaden*. News of "Lenore" spread like wildfire and as soon as it was published, it was immediately translated into several languages, including English, French, Italian, Portuguese, Dutch, Russian, Polish, and even Latin. One translation and adaptation of "Lenore" into English became Sir Walter Scott's first major work (Häntzschel and Häntzschel 1987, 1210).

From April until September 1773, Bürger worked on "Lenore," which was published in 1774 in the *Göttinger Musenalmanach*. Bürger's major sources for this ballad included a folk song that he claimed to have heard from a servant girl; Herder's "Auszug aus einem Briefwechsel über Ossian und die Lieder alter Völker"; Thomas Percy's ballad, "Sweet William's Ghost"; Goethe's *Götz von Berlichingen*; and Johann Christian Günther's poem, "An Leonore" (To Lenora; Häntzschel and Häntzschel 1987, 1212). A more distant, indirect, and hitherto underappreciated influence on the ballad is the popularity of the vampire phenomenon at the time Bürger wrote the ballad.

Bürger claimed to have obtained the material for this story from a folksong he heard from a servant girl, but he also emphasized the originality of his *Kunstballade* (art ballad). Considering the influences that folksongs had on poets at the time, especially after Herder's publication of the "Auszug aus einem Briefwechsel über Ossian und die Lieder alter Völker" (Excerpt from Letters about Ossian and the Folksongs of Ancient Peoples), the excitement that Bürger displayed at having adapted this folksong is understandable. There is, however, some doubt among scholars about the authenticity of the folksong that Bürger claimed to have heard (Schmidt-Kaspar 1986, 224). It is widely believed that the apparent discovery of this song through the idyllic setting of the "Spinnstube" (spinning wheel room) was in fact a creation by Bürger in order to strengthen the claim of the ballad's popular appeal and its origin in folklore, predating the comparably manufactured "folk traditions" of the Romantic period.

Independent of one another, August Wilhelm Schlegel (1767–1845) and Ludwig Uhland (1787–1862) supported Bürger's claims about the originality of his ballad, and the degree to which it is based on the northern European legend of Lenore, respectively.[8] In 1797 Schlegel published a short essay, "Noch ein Wort über die Originalität von Bürgers Lenore" (One more statement on the originality of Bürger's "Lenore") in the journal *Neuer Teutscher Merkur*, in which he refers to a conversation he had with Bürger during which Bürger explained that he had learned of the Lenore folksong from a friend and that she only remembered selected verses of the song.

In 1832, Ludwig Uhland wrote a short essay titled "Aufsatz über den Sagenstoff zu Gottfried August Bürgers Ballade 'Lenore'" (Essay on the Source Material for Gottfried August Bürger's Ballad "Lenore"), which was published a year later in the *Kritische Blätter der Börsenhalle*. In the essay, Uhland explains the origins and the plot of the story and mentions that the story had been told since the mid-seventeenth century and that Bürger placed it approximately a hundred years later than the original story. According to Uhland, the original story, with its reference to a soldier from the Frisian army who died in Bohemia, takes place during the Thirty Years' War after the battle between Bohemia and Palatinate that ended in 1623. In his retelling of the story's plot, Uhland is able to demonstrate the significant changes that Bürger made to the story in order to adapt the folktale for his ballad and make it more relevant for his readers.

Bürger's "Lenore" had a particularly strong influence on British Gothic poets of the late eighteenth and the nineteenth centuries, such as Samuel Taylor Coleridge, Robert Southey, Lord Byron, and John Keats, who contributed significantly to turning the vampire into a literary phenomenon that has persisted and even increased in popularity ever since. Coleridge and Southey were directly influenced by "Lenore" and published the first vampire poems in British literature. In 1798, Coleridge published the first British poem with an aristocratic vampire, "Christabel," and in 1801 Southey published "Thalaba the Destroyer" (Melton 1999, 472). Coleridge published his poem before Southey published his, and while Coleridge's poem is widely accepted as a vampire poem, he never identified it as such. Considering that "Thalaba the Destroyer" is clearly a vampire poem, some actually credit Southey with introducing the vampire to British literature (Melton 1999, 576). Lord Byron and Keats were very enthusiastic about "Lenore." Spurred on by his enthusiasm for "Lenore," Lord Byron wrote the vampire poem, "The Giaour," which was published in 1813. Keats contributed two poems to early British vampire literature. His poem "La Belle Dame Sans Merci" (1819) is considered to be generally of outstanding quality. In 1820, he published a second poem with a vampire theme, "Lamia"; like Goethe's "Bride of Corinth," "Lamia" is based on the ancient Greek story of Menippus, recorded by Philostratus in his *Life of Apollonius of Tyana*, and is thus very likely influenced by Goethe's poem as well (Bunson 1993, 142). As an inspiration on an international scale to poets whose names are generally associated with the earliest vampire literature, Bürger's "Lenore" was fundamental to the introduction of the vampire theme into literature.

Sir Walter Scott produced one of four translations into English of Bürger's poem in 1796. His translation of "Lenore," along with another of Bürger's ballads, "Der wilde Jäger" (The Wild Huntsman) and Goethe's *Götz von Berlichingen* were Scott's first publications (Bunson 1993, 235; Schmidt-Kaspar 1986, 229). Scott published his translation of "Lenore" as "William and Helen" and "Der wilde Jäger" as "The Chase" after "William and Helen" had been circulated privately among the literary circles of his native Edinburgh. His translations of these poems were so highly regarded that he was encouraged to publish them, though he was quite reluctant to do so, because the translations had been intended to be circulated privately (Scott 1857, 155–56). In his translation of "Lenore," Scott maintained the passionate tone, very likely in part because he so admired Bürger and other *Sturm und Drang* (Storm and Stress) poets, such as Klopstock and the early works by Goethe and Schiller that belonged to this period. This admiration for the German poets is further evidenced by his translation of *Götz* (Barnaby n.d., "Biography"). Structurally, however, Scott divided Bürger's eight-line stanzas into four-line stanzas and numbered them throughout.[9] In addition to maintaining the general tone of the poem, Scott put much effort into his translation of Bürger's onomatopoeic expressions, which are so characteristic of his style. For example, Scott translates stanza 13 of "Lenore," marking Wilhelm's arrival at Lenore's door, as follows:

> Then crash! the heavy drawbridge fell
> That o'er the moat was hung;
> And clatter! clatter! on its boards
> The hoof of courser rung.
>
> The clank of echoing steel was heard
> As off the rider bounded;
> And slowly on the winding stair
> A heavy footstep sounded.
>
> And hark! and hark! a knock—Tap! Tap!
> A rustling stifled noise;
> Door-latch and tinkling staples ring—
> At length a whispering voice.[10]

These are stanzas 24–26 of Scott's translation. Bürger's original stanza 13 is as follows:

> But hark to the clatter and the pat pat patter!
> Of a horse's heavy hoof!
> How the steel clanks and rings as the rider springs!
> How the echo shouts aloof!
> While silently and lightly the gentle bell
> Tingles and jingles softly and well;
> And low and clear through the door plank thin
> Comes the voice without to the ear within:

Clearly, Scott allowed himself significant poetic license in his translation of this stanza in particular, but probably more importantly, as Bürger may have agreed, Scott maintained the popular appeal of the poem in the passionate tone of his translation and in the onomatopoeic language that he uses.

In other areas of his translation, Scott reveals more direct information about Wilhelm's likely nature as a vampire than is evident from the original German. For example, when Wilhelm begins to explain to Lenore why they must ride during the night, instead of waiting for daybreak in Bürger's stanza 15, Scott has him say the following (Scott's stanza 29):

> "We saddle late—from Hungary
> I rode since darkness fell;
> And to its bourne we both return
> Before the matin bell."

The equivalent stanza in Bürger's original mentions Bohemia, a region in the western part of the Czech Republic, instead of Hungary. Though Bürger's Wilhelm never specifically mentions that they must reach their destination by morning, he does imply that they must reach their destination that night in stanza 16: "An hundred miles must be ridden and sped / Ere we may lie down in the bridal-bed." Toward the end of the ballad, in stanza 28, there is another indirect indication that Wilhelm must reach the grave before dawn:

> Horse, horse! meseems 'tis the cock's shrill note,
> And the sand is well nigh spent;
> Horse, horse, away! 'tis the break of day,—
> 'Tis the morning air's sweet scent.

The effect of Wilhelm's indirect references to the fact that he must reach his destination, later revealed to be his grave, by dawn creates an atmosphere of suspense and uncertainty in Bürger's poem that nonetheless leaves no doubt as to Wilhelm's true nature as a vampire. Regardless of the occasional inconsistencies with Bürger's original poem, Scott's translation of "Lenore" was an immediate success, much like Bürger's original poem had been when it was published more than twenty years earlier.

Bürger viewed folklore, popular imagination, and superstition as essential resources that made it possible to appeal to people and to empathize with their emotions and concerns (Kaim-Kloock 1963, 175). Bürger's popular appeal is evident in this poem in the extreme language, the strong expressions, and the onomatopoeic words. Throughout the entire poem there are examples of repeated desperate expletives such as "Help, Heaven, help," "Oh!" "Oh mother, mother!" "O woe!" "Alas!" and so on. The onomatopoeic words begin with Wilhelm's appearance in stanza 13 and have the effect of making the eerie atmosphere of the central part of the ballad decidedly more vivid. Onomatopoeic expressions such as "pat pat patter," "tingles and jingles" (stanza 13), "hush hush hush" (stanza 26), effectively lend a vivid folk song quality to the poem and only occur in connection with Wilhelm and the ghosts in the cemetery. Consequently, these onomatopoeic expressions emphasize the folklore quality of the supernatural element in the poem and draw attention to a very important part of folk belief—superstition. By including folk belief and superstition in the story of this ballad, Bürger adhered to the tendency of *Sturm and Drang* poets to emphasize the importance of human imagination (Kaim-Kloock 1963, 175). These poets saw it as their goal to express feelings as accurately as possible. Bürger achieved this goal in his integration of a story from folklore with contemporary history, and through his use of a language derived directly from the people (Karthaus 1976, 17).

In his famous review of Bürger's poetry, "Über Bürgers Gedichte" (Bürger's Poems), which was published in 1791 in the *Allgemeine Literatur-Zeitung*, Schiller harshly criticized Bürger's skills as a poet and his famous ballad. Despite his harsh criticism of Bürger's focus on popular appeal in his poetry, Schiller was very likely influenced by Bürger's poems "Lenore" and "Der wilde Jäger" among others when he wrote his play *Rosamund oder die Braut der Hölle* (Rosamund or the Bride of Hell), which remained a fragment and was written either in 1800 or 1804 (Koopmann 1998, 535). Regarding his review of Bürger's work, however, it is important to bear in mind that Schiller's purpose with the review was to establish an ideal standard for poetry with an ideal reader in mind. In his poetry and his theory on aesthetics, Schiller sought to apply generally valid rules to literature, in order to establish a classical aesthetic ideal concerning literature and the poet who produces that literature. Bürger, however, considered himself a *Volksdichter* (folk poet), a popular poet who reflected the concerns and experiences of the populace in his work. In this regard, he compared himself to Homer. In his critique of Bürger and his work, Schiller used Bürger's goal of producing poetry in the tradition established by Homer to show that this is no longer possible, because *das Volk*, a virtually homogenous entity, no longer existed toward the end of the eighteenth century in Germany. Schiller was referring here to the social hierarchy or *Ständegesellschaft*, and the numerous principalities that did not allow for homogeneity in Bürger's sense of the *Dichter des Volkes* (poet of the people); Schiller saw Bürger as a poet with clear potential, for whom popularity is extremely important (Koopmann 1998, 720). With comments such as this one, however, Schiller does not necessarily intend to conclude that the *Volksdichter* per se has no place anymore, but rather that the modern *Volksdichter* cannot disregard the educated classes, as he claims Bürger does with his poetry. Specifically, he states that the modern *Volksdichter* cannot simply make it easy for himself, disregarding the approval of the educated classes and exclusively adapting himself to the potential understanding by the masses (Koopmann 1998, 720). Schiller seems truly disappointed that a poet with Bürger's potential would compromise his integrity and genius by appealing to the masses as he does in his poetry (Wirsich-Irwin 1992, 81). Bürger wanted to be judged on his own principles, and in so doing, he practiced a much more modern type of criticism that hinted at what would follow in the nineteenth century (Koopmann 1982, 165). Unfortunately, Bürger could not know how modern his notions of literary criticism were, and so Schiller's critique devastated him.

Storm and Stress literature, such as Bürger's "Lenore," typically demonstrates strong tendencies toward social criticism. In this particular poem, religion and war are viewed in a critical light. Bürger's purpose with "Lenore," however, was neither to preserve the tradition surrounding religious faith nor to predict its demise. Instead, he aimed to demonstrate that the religiously dogmatic faith, represented by the mother's unwavering devotion to God, is no longer sufficient to console her daughter. In this ballad, war is shown to be a mere whim by two rulers, specifically the Prussian King Frederick the Great and the Austro-Hungarian Empress Maria Theresa, with dire consequences for the people. The war comes to an immediate end as soon as these rulers decide to end it, simply because they tire of it, according to Bürger (stanza 2):

> The Empress and the Kin
> With ceaseless quarrel tired,
> At length relaxed the stubborn hate
> Which rivalry inspired:

In this poem, Wilhelm is the dead lover who returns in order to take his mourning fiancée with him after she has renounced God and pledged herself to death in her desire to be with her deceased lover. This motif is an ancient one, common throughout Europe in folk songs, fairy tales, and legends as it connects excessive mourning for the dead and love or even lust for the dead with the universal taboo of necrophilia. The connection to necrophilia is especially evident in the motif of the dead lover returning that prevails in the earliest vampire poems. Bürger, however, takes this motif and adds very new elements to it in his ballad (Schmidt-Kaspar 1986, 221). One of Bürger's innovations for the genre of the *Kunstballade* is placing the story of this ballad in recent contemporary history—in the Battle of Prague of 1757, which took place during the Seven Years' War (1756–1763). Bürger and his contemporaries could easily recall the Seven Years' War and the return of the soldiers who fought in the battles.[11] Wilhelm returns from the Battle of Prague as a revenant with the intent of taking his fiancée to her death. At the same time, the fact that Wilhelm returns from a central European country as a vampire reflects the contemporary association of the vampire phenomenon with central Europe. Bürger lived in Halle when he was a boy, and probably experienced the Prussian army's return from the battle in much the same way that he describes it in the poem. In addition to choosing a recent war as a setting for his ballad, to which his contemporaries could relate, Bürger has the soldiers return from a battle that took place in the part of the world that western Europe associated the vampire superstition. When tracing the vampire in German literature, it is significant that the first two vampire poems by Ossenfelder and Bürger directly associate their vampire characters with central European countries. The fact that Wilhelm has come from Bohemia, which he reveals to Lenore in stanza 15, reflects early characteristics of vampires regarding their geographic origins, and coincides with information from the numerous reports of vampires that had been circulating in Europe for approximately forty years by the time Bürger wrote his poem. It is true that these reports usually situated the vampire in Hungary, Serbia, or Romania rather than Bohemia, but Bürger's mention of Bohemia in conjunction with the vampire has a dual purpose in this ballad of combining contemporary history with the history of the central European vampire.

A second innovation that Bürger brings to the *Kunstballade* as a genre of poetry is the transformation of the characters in the poem from mere schematic types, common in folklore, fairy tales, and legends, to well-defined characters with distinct historical and social backgrounds. Lenore is a simple young woman who was raised by her mother as a devout Christian and whose fiancé died in the war. Her situation is representative of the lives and losses of many women and families during this time. Finally, Bürger adds a third element to the folklore motif of the woman mourning the death of a lover, who returns to take her with him. In contrast to most folksongs, Bürger does not conceive of the dead lover's appearance on the scene as the belated fulfillment of true love, but rather as a punishment for the sin that Lenore commits through her excessive and blasphemous grief (Schmidt-Kaspar 1986, 221).

In his ballad, Bürger also combined essential elements of Storm and Stress poetry, such as passion and a focus on the emotions rather than cool reason, in a ballad that intended to address the entirety of human experience. The story of this ballad refers to the great topics of literature, indeed to human life and torment as such: love, death, faith, despair, and punishment. In his poem, Bürger gives a voice to folklore, popular imagination, and superstition in the form of the revenant by focusing on a variation of one of the greatest superstitions associated with vampires specifically and revenants in general—namely, the potential consequences of abandoning one's faith. It is the story about a young woman whose fiancé does not return from the war, specifically the Battle of Prague during the Seven Years' War. It is already clear in the first stanza that she fears that he has died, because she has not heard from him in such a long time. Her fears are confirmed when she cannot find him among the soldiers who are returning from the war. Here, Lenore's punishment for abandoning her faith is that she is killed by a vampire who is none other than her fallen fiancé. In stark contrast to the woman in Ossenfelder's poem, who is to be punished for her strong religious faith, Bürger's Lenore is punished by death for her rejection of faith. In Bürger's ballad, Lenore reacts entirely on her passion and undying love for her fallen fiancé, Wilhelm. Her rebellion against God is based entirely on her emotions. For Storm and Stress poets, this inclusion of people's feelings and passions was essential in order to portray a complete image of the human condition, and it allowed the poet to show a person in his or her individual totality. In order to do this, the poet had to consider all aspects that made up human beings. This included feelings, passions, imagination, irrational behavior, and spontaneous reactions to situations, even if they opposed all reason (Kaiser 1976, 184). In Storm and Stress poetry, a person's emotions and passions do not exist in opposition to his or her ability to reason, but rather they are accepted as an integral part of human expression, indeed of the human condition as such. Remembering that vampire stories were brought to Germany partly through scientific, ethnographic, and medical treatises, we can glimpse the dialectical process whereby reason and science produce the opposite, a world of the supernatural and of strong emotion where Bürger's passionate character Lenore is the hero, rather than a character such as Lessing's rational-thinking Nathan in his play, *Nathan, the Wise*.

Lenore's bitter despair over Wilhelm's likely death reaches a climax in a passionate dialogue with her mother that accounts for seven stanzas, specifically stanzas 5 through 11, of the total thirty-two stanzas. To her mother's horror, Lenore renounces her faith in God and expresses her wish to die, because she believes that Wilhelm has fallen. In stanza 5, she responds to her mother's cry for God's mercy by stating that he shows no mercy:

> Her mother clasped her tenderly
> With soothing words and mild:
> "My child, may God look down on thee,—
> God comfort thee, my child."
> "Oh! mother, mother! gone is gone!
> I reck no more how the world runs on:
> What pity to me does God impart?
> Woe, woe, woe! for my heavy heart!"

The following stanzas consist of Lenore's sudden and determined rebellion against God because Wilhelm did not return from the war, despite her mother's attempts to console her and put a halt to her rejection of faith (stanza 6):

> "Help, Heaven, help and favour her!
> Child, utter an Ave Marie!
> Wise and great are the doings of God;
> He loves and pities thee."
> "Out, mother, out, on the empty lie!
> Doth he heed my despair,—doth he list to my cry?
> What boots it now to hope or to pray?
> The night is come,—there is no more day."

In this explosive dialogue between mother and daughter, which might strike some readers as merely delaying the "real" plot with Wilhelm, Bürger reveals the mother's religiously dogmatic faith as no longer fundamental. Bürger shows here how Lenore's passion now belongs entirely to Wilhelm, where before it belonged to God. At the end of this dialogue, the mother fears punishment by God, because Lenore rejects her faith as a result of how intensely she mourns the loss of her fallen fiancé. Lenore does not want to continue living without Wilhelm. She cannot and does not want to find consolation in God.

In stanza 9, Lenore's despair reaches a climax after her mother tries to reason with her. In this stanza, she expresses her desire for death and her rejection of her faith:

> "Oh! mother, mother! gone is gone,
> And lost will still be lost!
> Death, death is the goal of my weary soul,
> Crushed and broken and crost.
> Spark of my life! down, down to the tomb:
> Die away in the night, die away in the gloom!
> What pity to me does God impart?
> Woe, woe, woe! for my heavy heart!"

After her argument with her mother, Lenore continues to despair into the night, when she hears someone arrive at her door. For the rest of the day and into the night she is in utter despair over his death. Indeed, Lenore equates her dearly beloved Wilhelm very straightforwardly with her own purpose in life (stanza 11):

> "My mother, what is happiness?
> My mother, what is Hell?
> With William is my happiness,—
> Without him is my Hell!
> Spark of my life! down, down to the tomb:
> Die away in the night, die away in the gloom!
> Earth and Heaven, Heaven and earth,
> Reft of William are nothing worth."

In its most basic form, literary dialogue is simply the written representation of a conversation between two or more people that can take on one of two forms: enlightened or empty dialogue (Daemmrich and Daemmrich 1987, 86; Schaeffer 1988, 387). Enlightened dialogue exists when the conversation between two or more people serves to move the action along or can convey characteristics of the speakers that identify their individual personalities and the relationships they have with one another (Daemmrich and Daemmrich 1987, 85). The motif of empty dialogue is at the opposite end of the spectrum from enlightened dialogue. For example, while enlightened dialogue functions to identify the characters who are speaking and their relationships with one another, empty dialogue underscores the inability of people to form meaningful relationships. In literature, empty dialogue is often constructed by employing numerous repetitions and the frequent use of clichés in an effort to demonstrate how language can be noncommunicative and reflect the emptiness of human interaction. Though silence is the natural role of the listener in a conversation, thus functioning as an essential part of enlightened dialogue, it has also been employed in literature to negate the role that dialogue usually plays. Hence, silence in a conversation or in lieu of conversation can be used to imply the inability of language to convey certain feelings, especially feelings of horror or confusion. As the negation of dialogue, silence can also function to indicate the breakdown of the relationship between the intended speakers (Daemmrich and Daemmrich 1987, 88). To adapt terminology from motif studies, the dialogue between mother and daughter in Bürger's "Lenore" is "enlightened" because it advances the action, the speakers respond to one another, the dialogue identifies personal characteristics, and it reveals the state of the relationship the speakers have with each other. This dialogue extends for seven stanzas, beginning with stanza 5. From the first exchange between mother and daughter in stanza 5, their personal character traits are revealed as they respond to one another. It is clear from the start of their conversation that the mother has a very strong religious faith when she says: "My child, may God look down on thee" after she sees her daughter's despair over not finding Wilhelm among the soldiers returning from war. Lenore's willingness to reject God and the ease with which she is able to reject her faith is immediately evident in her reply to her mother's call for God's mercy: "What pity to me does God impart?"

This brief exchange lays the groundwork for the character development that intensifies throughout the course of the dialogue. For example, the mother's character trait as a devout Christian is identified more intensely in the following stanza (stanza 6):

> "Help, Heaven, help and favour her!
> Child, utter an Ave Marie!
> Wise and great are the doings of God;
> He loves and pities thee."

This accompanies an equal intensification of Lenore's rejection of God and her faith in the same stanza:

> "Oh! mother, mother! gone is gone!
> I reck no more how the world runs on:
> What pity to me does God impart?
> Woe, woe, woe! for my heavy heart!"

This exchange continues in like fashion in stanza 7, employing the same dialogue structure as in stanzas 5 and 6; the mother preaches to her daughter and Lenore defiantly rejects God. For the remainder of the dialogue, Bürger devotes a stanza apiece to the mother and to Lenore. After her attempts to preach God's mercy to her daughter fail in stanzas 6 and 7, the mother offers an alternative to Wilhelm's probable death in stanza 8, in a desperate attempt to calm her daughter and possibly restore her faith. She suggests that Wilhelm might have stayed behind and married another woman:

> What if the traitor's false faith failed,
> By sweet temptation tried,—
> What if in distant Hungary
> He clasp another bride?—

Lenore's despair intensifies further in stanza 9, to the point that she desires death and Wilhelm in death. Without Wilhelm, her life is not worth living. After her mother makes a final attempt to turn her back to her faith in stanza 10, Lenore repeats her death wish and her rejection of faith for eternal life in heaven after death, word for word at the end of their dialogue in stanza 11: "Earth and Heaven, Heaven and earth, / Reft of William are nothing worth."

The next dialogue in the ballad is between Lenore and Wilhelm, and it begins when a man on horseback arrives at Lenore's door in stanza 13. His identity as Wilhelm is not revealed until the next stanza, when Lenore clearly recognizes him standing at her door. He wants to take Lenore with him, but she prefers that he come into the house because it is stormy outside. His answer to this request, "I must not stay," makes him seem strange to the reader for the first time (Schöne 1980, 180). He finally manages to convince Lenore to travel one hundred miles "to the bridal-bed." Despite her doubts about embarking on a long trip by horseback in the night, and her questions about the wedding and the place where they will live, she jumps on his horse and leaves with him. For most of the remainder of the poem, the ride on horseback has the dual effect of building suspense and intensifying the supernatural atmosphere of the poem. To this end, the horse or "ghost rider" motif plays a very important role.

Animals have always played important roles in myths, fairy tales, and other fantastic literature with the purpose of emphasizing certain characteristics, such as flying, cunning, or superhuman strength. In antiquity the gods often transformed themselves into animals in order to seduce humans.[12] Conversely, the transformation of human beings into animal form in modern literature often signified the conscious decision on the part of the person undergoing the transformation to reject his or her humanity in favor of a more primal, animal nature.[13] Numerous allegories, fairy tales, and fables feature animals that function as metaphors for human behavior. To name only a few examples, the fox and the wolf usually represent trickery and cunning, the bird typically represents freedom and creativity, and the snake often represents evil and seduction. In addition to its common application as a metaphor for human behavior or aspirations, the animal motif in literature often functions to support themes, such as wild nature, that do not include human beings or are even beyond human comprehension, namely the supernatural or the demonic.

The motif of the horse in particular usually adds a unique perspective to the theme of uncontrollable nature, because this animal is often presented in literature as itself wild and unpredictable, despite its long domestication by human beings (Daemmrich and Daemmrich 1987, 32–33). This presumed unpredictable nature of the horse, which is often destructive, not only reflects the uncontrollable forces of nature, but also the unpredictable and extreme emotions of the people who ride them and their struggles with their inner demons (Daemmrich and Daemmrich 1987, 33).[14] The predominance of the horse motif in "Lenore" is closely associated with the vampire Wilhelm. It is not surprising, however, that the horse is the only animal that is associated with the vampire in this early vampire ballad, if the folklore that inspired it is taken into consideration. In central European folklore and superstition, the horse is closely associated with the vampire as one means of determining the presence of a vampire in a grave, aside from the actual exhumation and close investigation of the body of the suspected vampire. In Hungarian folklore, for example, one of the most common methods of detecting a vampire in a cemetery is to lead a horse of solid color over all the graves in a cemetery. It was believed that the horse would refuse to step over the grave in which a vampire is buried. The horse and the child riding it should both be virgins according to this folklore, and it was also important that the horse had never stumbled (McNally and Florescu 1994, 122). This particular method of detecting vampires is not restricted to Hungary, but varies regionally. In some central European folklore accounts, the horse must be either solid white or solid black in color, and may or may not be ridden by a virgin; not all folklore requires that the horse had never stumbled (Barber 2010, 68–69).

The vampire of folklore rarely demonstrated the ability to transform into certain animals, but was sometimes associated with animals such as werewolves, that were in fact defined by their ability to transform from human to animal form. The association of the vampire with the werewolf very likely originated from the fact that the same word, *upir*, or a regional variation thereof, was applied to both creatures in central Europe. In Chinese superstition, however, the *chiang-shih* are vampires that can actually transform into wolves, rather than being merely associated with werewolves, as they were in central Europe. In addition to its association with shape-changing animals, the vampire of central European superstition was believed to prey on livestock as well as on human beings (Melton 1999, 15). Any unexplained or sudden deaths of cattle or other livestock in a village were attributed to vampire activity, just as unexplained or sudden human deaths were blamed on vampires.

The empusae of Greek mythology demonstrate physical animal traits of the donkey and the female dog in order to emphasize certain negative characteristics associated with these animals in mythology that can also be applied to human beings. Bram Stoker re-invented the vampire's association with shape-changers, such as werewolves, by providing his vampire with the actual ability to transform into a wolf or a bat in addition to his general association with and command of animals in his novel, *Dracula* (1897). In this novel, Dracula exhibits animal traits in his ability to climb down a wall of his castle, face down, like a lizard or an insect.[15] He is also able to command wolves that function as his helpers.[16] Though these animal traits and the ability to command animals reflect much of the folklore surrounding the vampire, Dracula's ability to actually transform into certain animals, such as a bat or a large dog, is the innovation that Stoker brought to the literary vampire in the late nineteenth century.[17] Whereas the modern literary vampire since Stoker's *Dracula* demonstrates the ability to transform into or command the wolf and the bat, and he may display certain characteristics of these animals, such as the enlarged canine teeth that leave small puncture wounds, the earliest literary vampires from folklore and the German ballads did not demonstrate these characteristics. For the most part, the vampires in the first German ballads had little or no association with animals that was in any way supernatural. In this, they closely resembled the vampires from central European folklore.

In Bürger's ballad, the horse carries Wilhelm and Lenore to their grave with increasing speed that ultimately surpasses what is natural and accounts for most of the action and suspense in the ballad. The threefold increase in the pace of the ride, reflecting the threefold increase in Lenore's fear, is a prime example of how the horse motif functions to reflect the emotions of the rider and how the horse literally carries its rider into supernatural realms. Though the horse in Bürger's ballad does not have the traditional purpose from folklore of aiding in the detection of a vampire, Bürger nevertheless associates the horse with the vampire, the graveyard, and supernatural speed.

During Wilhelm's and Lenore's ride on horseback, there is a threefold acceleration of the question-and-answer game between them that parallels the increase of the pace of the ride. The unnatural manner of Wilhelm's participation in the dialogue is most noticeable in his repeated questions to Lenore. In stanzas 20, 24, and 27 he asks the same question with the exact same wording and the same indicated level of excitement:

> "What ails my love? the moon shines bright:
> Bravely the dead men ride through the night.
> Is my love afraid of the quiet dead?"

Lenore's answers to Wilhelm's questions about whether or not she is frightened of the dead become increasingly anxious and fearful. In stanza 20, she simply says "Ah! no;—let them sleep in their dusty bed!" In stanza 24, she is already a bit more fearful and says: "Ah! let them alone in their dusty bed!" In stanza 27, she is even more frightened: "Alas! let them alone in their dusty bed!" The increase in the intensity of her fear demonstrates her humanity, in contrast to Wilhelm's unnatural demeanor. At the same time, the ride becomes increasingly fast and supernatural until a climax is reached at the cemetery. In stanza 20, the pace of the ride is still very realistic:

> Here to the right and there to the left
> Flew fields of corn and clover,
> And the bridges flashed by to the dazzled eye,
> As rattling they thundered over.

In stanza 24, the ride has already become physically impossible:

> How flew to the right, how flew to the left,
> Trees, mountains in the race!
> How to the left, and the right and the left,
> Flew town and market-place!

In stanza 27, the heavens and the stars fly past. Here the ride has been accelerated to its fastest and most unnatural pace:

> How flew the moon high overhead,
> In the wild race madly driven!
> In and out, how the stars danced about,

And reeled o'er the flashing heaven!

Upon their arrival at the cemetery, Wilhelm's clothing falls off and he is revealed as a skeleton with an hourglass and a scythe—as a vampire disguised as the Grim Reaper. Lenore dies, and the ghosts in the cemetery speak the didactic finale of the ballad in stanza 32 (Schöne 1980, 181):

> "Patience, patience, when the heart is breaking;
> With thy God there is no question-making:
> Of thy body thou art quit and free:
> Heaven keep thy soul eternally!"

In contrast to Lenore's increased anxiety during the ride on horseback, Wilhelm's questions are repeated word for word, with no indication of any change in expression or emotion. In addition to this simple lack of emotion, Wilhelm does not make any effort to calm Lenore or relieve her of her anxieties. Instead he is preoccupied with death and with the dead, in his questions to Lenore and elsewhere in the ballad. For example, just after they begin riding to the "bridal chamber," they pass a funeral procession, which is described in some detail in stanza 21. Stanza 22 consists of Wilhelm's spoken response to and keen interest in the funeral procession and of simultaneous references to his betrothal to Lenore:

> "You bury your corpse at the dark midnight,
> With hymns and bells and wailing;
> But I bring home my youthful wife
> To a bride-feast's rich regaling.
> Come, chorister, come with thy choral throng,
> And solemnly sing me a marriage-song;
> Come, friar, come,—let the blessing be spoken,
> That the bride and the bridegroom's sweet rest be unbroken."

In the poem, Wilhelm's lack of emotion is very conspicuous, especially against the backdrop of Lenore's excessive passion. As a prominent figure in a Storm and Stress poem, Wilhelm's lack of passion is very suspicious and is an early indication that he may not be human, since he does not demonstrate this very basic human characteristic that was important to Storm and Stress poets. Though it may initially seem that the dialogue between Wilhelm and Lenore during their ride is relatively empty because of the repetitiveness of Wilhelm's questions and his inability or unwillingness to respond to Lenore's fear, his unnatural manner of speaking in the dialogue builds suspense, by causing the reader to be curious about his general nature, which is revealed at the end. In fact, it is precisely this unnatural manner of speaking that defines Wilhelm's character as unnatural. The dialogue between the two lovers is enlightened, based on the fact that it reveals information about the characters and adds to the suspense in the ballad by paralleling the increasingly unusual pace of the ride. Wilhelm's role in the dialogue, however, is empty because of his inability or unwillingness to respond to her, but at the same time his uncanny communicative skills add to the unnatural atmosphere of the poem during this ride on horseback.

The lack of emotion on Wilhelm's part when he repeats his questions to Lenore, and his preoccupation with death, indicate three possible explanations for his strange behavior: he is Death disguised as Wilhelm; he is a ghost; or he is "undead," a vampire disguised as Wilhelm and Death. An argument for Wilhelm's true nature as Death disguised as Wilhelm can be based on the fact that he actually takes off his clothing in stanza 30 and reveals that his body is a skeleton. His head becomes a bare skull, and he is holding the Grim Reaper's scythe and hourglass:

> But see! But see! in an eyelid's beat,
> Towhoo! a ghastly wonder!
> The horseman's jerkin, piece by piece,
> Dropped off like brittle tinder!
> Fleshless and hairless, a naked skull,
> The sight of his weird head was horrible;
> The lifelike mask was there no more,
> And a scythe and a sandglass the skeleton bore.

On the other hand, a strong argument against his possible identity as Death in disguise is the fact that he is restricted to act at a certain time during the night and must return with Lenore to his coffin quickly. He makes his urgency clear in stanza 16:

> "Thro' the hawthorn-bush let whistle and rush,—
> Let whistle, child, let whistle!
> Mark the flash fierce and high of my steed's bright eye,
> And his proud crest's eager bristle.
> Up, up and away! I must not stay:
> Mount swiftly behind me! up, up and away!
> An hundred miles must be ridden and sped
> Ere we may lie down in the bridal-bed."

Bürger's depiction of Death as a rider with an hourglass, a scythe, and a skull, as well as the ideas that a violent or untimely death does not allow the dead to rest in peace and that excessive mourning of surviving loved ones disturbs the peace of the dead, come directly from folklore (Grimm 1988, 84). But Wilhelm is not just Death in this ballad; he is in fact a vampire. In folklore a person was believed to return as a vampire under conditions very similar to those when Death would appear as a rider.

Death is neither restricted to a number of hours at night during which he can perform his duties, nor does he have to return to a coffin by a certain hour, as vampires do. But could Wilhelm be a ghost? He appears to Lenore as her fiancé whom she can touch, not as a disembodied, ethereal, and transparent spirit. In stanza 19 she puts her arms around him as they begin to ride:

"And gently smiling, with a sweet beguiling, / Her white hands clasped his waist." The German word *Gespenst* is a generic term that is applied to all supernatural beings, including ghosts, vampires, and werewolves. The word *Geist*, however, is used for ghosts in the sense of spirits that haunt certain places (Brittnacher 1994, 27). Hence, Wilhelm is a *Gespenst*, a supernatural being, when he reveals himself to be a skeleton with a scythe and an hourglass under his clothing at the end of the ballad, but he is not a ghost; the dead lover who returns for his lover in this ballad is a vampire. To the modern reader, it may not be immediately clear that Wilhelm is in fact a vampire, though there is no doubt that he is a dead lover returning for his beloved by the end of the poem. The modern reader's understanding of characteristics that define a vampire have been obfuscated by the strong influence that nineteenth-century British authors' embellishments of the literary vampire have had on twentieth- and twenty-first-century perceptions of the vampire. Wilhelm does not suck the blood of his beloved; he is never referred to as a vampire, and he is not staked in the end. Sucking blood was not always the folkloric vampire's preferred method of killing his kin; in fact, it was very likely a literary invention for dramatic and gruesome effect. The typical folkloric vampire usually smothered his victims, or caused a horrible epidemic in his village that came to an end only when the vampire met his.

Characteristics that identify Wilhelm's nature as a vampire rather than a mere ghost or the Grim Reaper in this ballad, and that connect him to central European folklore and superstition, are as follows: 1) the vampire appears bodily to his loved one(s), though it is clear that he has died; 2) he returns for his loved one with amorous intent; 3) he must return to his coffin; 4) he must do this at night, that is, before sunrise; and 5) he is not allowed to enter the home of the loved one for whom he returns (Melton 1999, 95). Evidence supporting Wilhelm's identity as a vampire masked as Death reflects these characteristics. First, he appears to Lenore in bodily form at night, and there is no doubt in her mind that he is Wilhelm. The vampire of folklore always appeared in human form to his loved ones at night as they slept. The vampire's human appearance sets him apart from other supernatural monsters, such as the ghost or the werewolf. Second, Wilhelm cannot cross the threshold into Lenore's house. It is a common belief in vampire lore, though not universal, that this malicious revenant cannot enter a home, or often not unless he is invited.[18] Third, Wilhelm does not appear to Lenore during the witching hour between midnight and one o'clock, as is the case for most ghosts of folklore, but rather he can only saddle his horse at this time. He tells Lenore in stanza 15, "Till the dead midnight we saddled not." In stanza 16, he explains that he has to return with her and cover one hundred miles that night. He cannot leave whenever he wants, and he is compelled to return with her by a certain hour. This is typical of vampires in central European folklore. Fourth, and probably most convincingly indicative of Wilhelm's nature as a vampire, he not only has an appointment to make at a certain time of the night, but his destination is predetermined as well. Wilhelm has to return to his coffin. When Wilhelm provides a detailed description of the "bridal chamber" in stanza 18, it becomes undeniably clear that he is in fact a vampire:

> "Ah! where is the chamber, William dear,
> And William, where is the bed?"
> "Far, far from here: still, narrow, and cool:
> Plank and bottom and lid."

Wilhelm is describing a coffin to his betrothed, and of all the supernatural monsters imaginable, only a vampire is compelled to return to his coffin, according to central European superstition. Furthermore, Wilhelm does not necessarily *want* to take her there; as a true vampire, he *must* and he is pressed for time (stanza 16): "An hundred miles must be ridden and sped / Ere we may lie down in the bridal-bed."

Though most supernatural creatures from folklore and literature are nocturnal, this has not always been true for vampires, especially in literature. In fact, the completely nocturnal nature of the fictional vampire and the exposure to sunlight as a means of actually destroying a vampire was an innovation by Friedrich Murnau in his film, *Nosferatu*, from 1922 (Melton 1999, 593). In eighteenth- and nineteenth-century British literature most of the vampires, such as the ones featured in Samuel Taylor Coleridge's poem, "Christabel" (1798), John Polidori's short story, "The Vampyre" (1819), James Malcolm Rymer's novel, *Varney the Vampyre* (1847), Sheridan Le Fanu's novella, *Carmilla* (1872), and Bram Stoker's *Dracula* (1897) could function during the day, but were sometimes weakened and tended to prefer the night. The German ballads by Bürger, Goethe, and Eichendorff, however, all feature nocturnal vampires. If we remember that the most popular vampire stories that came to western Europe in the early part of the eighteenth century[19] mainly featured nocturnal vampire activity, this is added support for the argument that the German poets were primarily influenced by central European folklore in their creation of the literary vampire. This, in turn, suggests that this nocturnal nature is a fundamental characteristic of the vampire that originated in the folklore and was modified later by British authors, possibly for dramatic effect and to underscore the vampire's ability to fit in among humans as a truly human-seeming monster.

JOHANN WOLFGANG VON GOETHE: "DIE BRAUT VON KORINTH" ("THE BRIDE OF CORINTH")

Goethe's vampire poem was first published in Friedrich Schiller's *Musenalmanach* in 1798 as a result of the two poets' combined efforts to produce classical ballad poetry in what has come to be known as their *Balladenjahr* (ballad year) in 1797. Goethe's source for "Die Braut von Korinth" was a classical Greek story recorded by Phlegon of Tralles during Roman Emperor Hadrian's reign (AD 76–138).[20] The original tale is a ghost story that Goethe combined with the vampire theme, with which he had been familiar since he was a young man. In fact, it is very likely that Goethe first became familiar with the vampire figure when the author Clemens Werthes visited him in Frankfurt in October 1774. Werthes had just translated a chapter of a book entitled *Viaggio in Dalmazia* by the Italian scientist and geographer, Abbate Alberto Fortis, and would go on to translate the entire book. In this particular chapter, "De costumi de' Morlacchi," which Werthes had just translated, Fortis discussed the customs of the Morlacks, a people from the Balkans, and their belief in vampires. Goethe based his poem, "Klaggesang der edlen Frauen des Asan Aga" (Lament of the noble women of Asan Aga; 1774/1775), on a Serbo-Croatian folksong that was included in this chapter of Fortis's book (Trunz 1988, 663). Goethe's familiarity with the vampire can thus at least be traced directly to this source. In his *Tagebuch* (diary), Goethe makes two separate references to his work on this ballad, in which he mentions that it is a poem with a vampire theme, thus directly indicating his familiarity with the vampire of superstition and folklore. Although there is no question about the bride's nature as a vampire, in part because Goethe referred to the ballad as a *vampyrisches Gedicht* (vampiric poem), he nevertheless only reveals her true nature in a very gradual and subtle manner until she finally explains her identity as a vampire to her mother at the end of the poem. This gradual revelation of the bride's monstrous identity is a common technique of increasing the suspense in a horror story.

The bride in this poem is dead—a revenant vampire—from the beginning, although the reader does not know this for sure until stanza 18, "But no heart is beating in her breast."[21] The bride and the young man in this ballad had been promised to one another at birth as a gesture of hospitality and friendship between the children's fathers. Later, the bride's family converted to Christianity, and in a moment of desperation her mother promised her daughter's service as a nun in return for the mother regaining her health after a long illness. The young woman only escapes from being confined to a nunnery through death. Though it is not clear how she dies, it is implied that she kills herself (stanza 23):

> "Mother! mother!"—Thus her wan lips say:
> "May not I one night of rapture share?
> From the warm couch am I chased away?
> Do I waken only to despair?
> It contents not thee
> To have driven me
> An untimely shroud of death to wear?"

This young woman returns as a monster, specifically as a vampire in Goethe's telling of the story in his ballad. Her return after death as a vampire supports the idea that she committed suicide, because this was a common fate of suicide victims in central European folklore.

The reader is first introduced to the bride in stanza 4, when she appears at the youth's door as he is falling asleep. She seems almost angelic in her modesty and appearance here in the beginning of the ballad, but reveals herself later to be a revenant who is driven to kill (Metzger 1994, 92). She apologizes for the intrusion, and wants to retreat. She has all the characteristics of a well-reared young lady in the Christian tradition to which her family had recently converted. For ten stanzas she resists the young man's approaches, and even provides hints that she is dead. In stanza 14, her hint is rather subtle:

> Now the ghostly hour of midnight knell'd,
> And she seem'd right joyous at the sign;
> To her pallid lips the cup she held,
> But she drank of nought but blood-red wine.
> For to taste the bread
> There before them spread,
> Nought he spoke could make the maid incline.

Though the mention of bread and wine is an obvious Christian reference, it is also a reference to antiquity. In Homer's *Odyssey*, for example, the living eat bread and the dead drink wine (Volckmann 1987, 159). In stanza 16, the bride's hint is more direct:

> And she comes, and lays her near the boy:
> "How I grieve to see thee sorrowing so!
> If thou think'st to clasp my form with joy,
> Thou must learn this secret sad to know;
> Yes! the maid, whom thou
> Call'st thy loved one now,
> Is as cold as ice, though white as snow."

The two make passionate love for the next four stanzas while the mother listens outside. The young man is not aware of his unintended necrophilia until the mother enters the room and the young woman reveals her true nature to her mother and blames her for it. Finally she begs her mother to dispose of her body in the proper manner by burning it. The ballad ends here without closure because it is not certain whether the mother grants her daughter this final wish.

In this ballad, the bride's character is ambiguous. She is at once innocent, "in veil and garment white array'd" (stanza 5), demure and restrained to such a degree that the young man recognizes her as his bride although he had not yet met her, and she is his downfall. Similarly, her white veil and gown hint at her dual identity as a bride and as a reanimated corpse dressed in a shroud.

In the end, Goethe's monster bride kills her fiancé because she is compelled as a vampire to do this until she is put to final rest. As a woman and as a vampire she is, in the words of Simone de Beauvoir in her book, *The Second Sex*, "everything that he is not [dead; a vampire] and that he longs for [his bride], his negation and his raison d'être" (de Beauvoir 1993, 162). As a woman, the bride is very likely physically capable of giving life, but as the *femme fatale* she destroys life. This aberration of the woman as "imagined woman" is reproduced here as a monster, the vampire who takes its victim's life-blood or energy.

The terms *femme fatale* or the *belle dame sans merci* are used "to describe a dangerous seductress who destroys the man who loves her" (Leavy 1988, 169). This figure is often portrayed as both seductive and monstrous, with the uncanny ability to seduce mortals into abandoning their usual responsibilities to their families and society. The *femme fatale* can appear in literature as a ruthless, malevolent character that maliciously seeks to destroy mortals, or as a pitiable character whose union with a certain man is motivated by a type of penance or curse that only the man can alleviate. Often the fatal woman is not only the aggressor, but also a victim or "the ambivalent combination of the sufferer who provokes anguish" (Daemmrich and Daemmrich 1987, 103). The *femme fatale* can be portrayed as either mortal or immortal.[22] She is a universal character in folklore and mythology that often appears in the form of a fairy, whether evil or not, who sometimes mates with humans, but whose influence on mortals is destructive. Examples of the *femme fatale* in western mythology include Lilith from Near Eastern mythology, the harpies, lamia and sirens from Greek mythology, and Celtic fairies, such as Morgaine. In Germany the *femme fatale* is the focal point in the folktales of Undine and Tannhäuser (Daemmrich and Daemmrich 1987, 103). Friedrich de la Motte Fouqué's novella, *Undine* (1811), is only one of many works in German literature that is based on the mythology of the *femme fatale* (Leavy 1988, 173–74).

As Christianity spread through Europe, many of these pagan fairies were relegated to the role of the evil seductress or temptress. For example, Venus, the goddess of love and beauty, became a malevolent temptress whose seduction of Tannhäuser caused his Christian soul to be condemned to hell (Daemmrich and Daemmrich 1987, 103). The malevolent traits of the *femme fatale* as the seductress who destroys her lover have resulted in the portrayal of this figure as a witch, a vampire, or a similar type of monster. The Greek lamia is an early example of the *femme fatale* who demonstrates vampire traits in her ruthless murder of mortal children.

Another characteristic of the *femme fatale* is that she is often dehumanized by exhibiting animal traits: Medusa has hair made of snakes, and the lamia changes shape from a snake to a woman. Additionally, she may appear as a ghost or a corpse, as is the case in Goethe's ballad, "The Bride of

Corinth." Another dehumanizing characteristic of the *femme fatale* occurs when she assumes the shape of a picture or a statue, as in Eichendorff's 1826 novella, *Das Marmorbild* (Daemmrich and Daemmrich 1987, 104–5). In addition to appearing in mythology and literature in conjunction with animal motifs, the *femme fatale* also appears in conjunction with places on earth that take on an otherworldly quality due to their remoteness or inaccessibility to the average mortal. These include the underwater world, mountaintops, and "the pleasure palace" (Daemmrich and Daemmrich 1987, 105). The underwater realm is common to the Undine folklore and the sirens in Homer's *Odyssey*, for example. In German literature, Goethe's ballad, "Der Fischer," Clemens Brentano's ballad, "Lore-Lay," and Heinrich Heine's poem, "Lore-Ley," are other examples of the connection between the *femme fatale* and life under water—certain death for the average mortal. The combination of the *femme fatale* with remote places such as mountaintops, mines, or other enclosed spaces from which her victims may never escape is evident in the Tannhäuser legend, Ludwig Tieck's *Rune Mountain* (1804), Thomas Mann's novel, *The Magic Mountain* (1924), and in the image of Lilith on the Brocken mountain in the "Walpurgis night" scene in Goethe's *Faust I*, to name a few.

The bride in Goethe's "The Bride of Corinth" is in fact the quintessential *femme fatale*. She is beautiful, erotic, seductive, destructive, and exotic. These extraordinary traits set the typical *femme fatale* apart from ordinary men and women to such an extent that she is elevated to the level of being what Virginia M. Allen calls "immortal, queen, goddess" in her book *The Femme Fatale: Erotic Icon* and thus the *femme fatale* is "less human" (1983, 4). Moreover, the full-blown *femme fatale* is self-determined and independent. She expresses the intent to destroy and is willfully malevolent; according to Allen, "she [. . .] indulges her sexuality without concern for her lover of the moment" (4). Though Goethe's vampire bride exhibits many of these essential traits of the *femme fatale*, she is neither self-determined, nor is she independent in her quest to destroy the young man. She explains herself quite clearly to her mother in stanza 26:

> From my grave to wander I am forc'd,
> Still to seek The Good's long-sever'd link,
> Still to love the bridegroom I have lost,
> And the life-blood of his heart to drink;
> When his race is run,
> I must hasten on,
> And the young must 'neath my vengeance sink.

As a vampire, the bride is compelled to rise from the grave to kill the lover whom she was denied in life; she is an active participant in his destruction, yet her good will before her transformation at the witching hour contradicts her actions. For this reason she is not a complete *femme fatale*. She is not self-determined or willful in the young man's destruction, and she does not act independently or intentionally. Though she tried to warn him several times, the young man does not (or chooses not to) understand her. As soon as the witching hour arrives, however, she must abandon any self-control or restraint that she might have exhibited previously and is compelled to indulge in her sexuality and ultimately kill her prey, which she had heretofore resisted. Hence, even though she exhibits the important trait of the *femme fatale* of wanton passion, it does not result from her will. She is as passive in death as she was in life, having been promised to a husband, converted to Christianity, and promised to the Church as a nun. She is even dependent upon others for her own final destruction, because she must beg her mother to destroy her body in a pagan ritual. The only indication of any active response on her part was her implied suicide.

The fact that the vampire in this poem is female sheds new light on Goethe's dual concept of the Eternal Feminine, which represents the "legendary confrontation of seductive evil and victimized innocent sweetness," the Mary/Eve dichotomy (Allen 1983, 20). In *Götz von Berlichingen* (1773), Goethe had already demonstrated the Eternal Feminine in the juxtaposition of two main characters: the demure Maria, and the destructive and manipulative seductress Adelheid. In *Faust* as well, the Eternal Feminine is represented by two separate characters: Gretchen, the innocent victimized girl, and Lilith, the epitome of the *femme fatale*. In "The Bride of Corinth," however, the dual concept of the Eternal Feminine is combined in one person. The bride in this ballad is initially reserved; in fact, she is almost angelic in her appearance and demure in her demeanor, warning the young man repeatedly, though indirectly, that she is a revenant. In the end, however, she cannot reconcile her love for the young man with her vampire nature, which compels her to kill him. As we have seen, the bride in this ballad is an incomplete vampire and an incomplete *femme fatale*. She is a vampire with a conscience who predates the virtuous vampire of the late twentieth century by almost two hundred years, and she is a *femme fatale* who has no will of her own or actual intent to destroy. The reader pities her and hopes that she will at least receive the final death that she requests in the end. In Goethe's imagination of the vampire bride in this poem, he shows that these two contrasting natures cannot coexist in one person and must result in the creation of a monster.

In his book, *Monster Theory: Reading Culture* (1996), Jeffrey Cohen offers the following explanation of what constitutes the monster and the monstrous in literature: "the monster is [. . .] a presence or absence that unsettles what has been constructed to be received as natural, as human" (ix). The vampire, with its ambiguous nature of being a human-seeming monster, is a particularly useful literary device for demonstrating the monstrous side of human nature. The dual concept of the Eternal Feminine as it is combined in one woman in Goethe's ballad is clearly a monstrous manifestation according to Cohen's definition of the monster. How can a vampire be, or even seem to be, virtuous based on contemporary and even more modern conceptualizations of the vampire?[23] The bride in this poem is not only an aberration of the imagined ideal woman because she exhibits characteristics of the *femme fatale* and the Eternal Feminine; as a vampire, she is also an aberration of the common conceptualization of the monster because she is a virtuous and pitiable monster, victimized and compelled to victimize others in turn. As such, she is essentially a dual monstrous Other.

As a woman and as a vampire the bride is a multifaceted and unique monster. She is at once the contemporary ideal woman in her beauty, her modesty, and her classically inspired composure as she faces her fate, yet she is a vampire and a *femme fatale* who is subject to an irreversible compulsion to kill the one she loves most. Although she is a vampire, she has a conscience. Though she exhibits traits of the *femme fatale*, her will is good. As befits a true literary monster, according to Cohen's definition, Goethe's bride is a mosaic of compelling and opposing characteristics that exist in one being, but cannot coexist. In her many conflicting parts she is truly a monster in a very modern sense that predates Mary Shelley's monster in her novel *Frankenstein; Or the Modern Prometheus* (1818). As such, Goethe's bride is a prime representative of the impossibility of the dual concept of the Eternal Feminine existing in one person. Because the woman is commonly associated with caring, self-sacrifice, and especially the ability to give life, Goethe's bride is particularly monstrous when she takes life instead. However destructively and monstrously this vampire bride behaves, by the end of the poem the reader feels compassion for her in her fate. This is only possible because she is not a complete *femme fatale*; in fact, she is an unintentional *femme fatale*. She is the passive participant in an act of destruction because she is compelled to kill. Women who become vampires later in the early nineteenth century, especially in British literature, are not always as innocent and pitiable as Goethe's bride.[24]

And though the bride must be killed in order for her to cease killing, the reader hopes that she may at least be put to rest in the manner she desires, in a pagan funeral pyre—the final vindication of a pagan life that had been destroyed by the dawn of a new age and a new religion. Goethe concludes his poem with the bride's plea to her mother to destroy her, and explains in detail how she should do this. The ending is unsettling, though, because the mother does not reply to her daughter's wish. This open ending does not provide any closure for the vampire bride or her victim and thus equally denies support for the established social order, represented by the mother, and for the vampire bride's rebellious challenge to her mother's authority (Metzger 1994, 93). From the nineteenth century through the present day, closure for the vampire, usually by the gruesome and symbolically loaded staking, has become a standard feature of vampire literature and film.

Considering that the intended readers of this poem were very likely familiar with the vampire stories and resulting debates, as well as with Bürger's "Lenore" by the time Goethe published his ballad, simply mentioning the common traits of the vampire rather than blatantly using the word, as Ossenfelder did in his poem, was enough to reveal the bride's identity as a vampire. The gradual progression of this revelation creates an atmosphere of suspense in the poem and reflects the novelty and ambiguous nature of the vampire as it was perceived in the eighteenth century.

"The Bride of Corinth" is set during the time of the Christianization of Corinth in the fifth century AD, and comments on the catastrophic results of forced conversion to Christianity in ancient Greece on a very personal level as the bride mourns the loss of her pagan culture (Trombley 1994, 295). In Goethe's ballad, Christianity is associated with cultural death; vampirism is the punishment for the suicide that the bride committed in response to forced conversion to Christianity rather than the punishment for excessive faith or lack thereof, as is the case in Ossenfelder's and Bürger's poems. In her existence as a revenant vampire and in her anger over a conversion to Christianity imposed on her by her mother, the bride in Goethe's ballad represents the "living death" of classical religion and culture in antiquity after Christianization, but also in its renaissance in Germany in the late eighteenth century. In stanza 9 the bride voices her discontent to the young man:

> From the house, so silent now, are driven
> All the gods who reign'd supreme of yore;
> One Invisible now rules in heaven,
> On the cross a Saviour they adore.
> Victims slay they here,
> Neither lamb nor steer,
> But the altars reek with human gore.

She is clearly angry that her family converted to Christianity, as she sees it as a religion that sacrifices human beings such as herself rather than animals. The youth does not know that his bride is dead until it is too late. He does, however, know that she and her family had converted to Christianity, and he is even concerned that he might not be welcome because he is still a pagan (stanza 2):

> But can he that boon so highly prized,
> Save 'tis dearly bought, now hope to get?
> They are Christians and have been baptized,
> He and all of his are heathens yet.

With these fears of the Unknown, the Other, still fresh on his mind, the young man begins to fall asleep when his bride appears to him. Later, in stanza 7, when he attempts to seduce the woman he recognizes as his bride, he mentions his pagan gods who can be associated with love, lust, greed, hedonism, and gluttony:

> "Stay, thou fairest maiden!" cries the boy,
> Starting from his couch with eager haste:
> "Here are Ceres', Bacchus' gifts of joy;
> Amor bringest thou, with beauty grac'd!
> Thou art pale with fear!
> Loved one let us here
> Prove the raptures the Immortals taste."

By mentioning these gods to her with the purpose of seducing her, the youth might be trying to save her from the monster he fears: Christianity. The most significant conflict in his mind is his desire for his bride and his simultaneous fear of her as the Other. She is what he is not. She is a woman, he is a man. She is a Christian and he is a pagan.

In this ballad, Goethe manages to weave together a variety of motifs under the general vampire theme. The bride represents the beliefs of a dying polytheistic Old World order that Goethe connects with the central European vampire superstition in the bride's identity as a revenant. This Old World is stuck in antiquity and can only clash self-destructively with the New World that is represented by the new monotheistic religion, Christianity, and her family's conversion to this new religion. The worlds of antiquity and modernity, represented in this poem by the reunion of the pagan lover and the bride, cannot coexist or be married, nor can a dying or dead antiquity (the bride) be satisfactorily reanimated in the modern world. The result is that the bride, a reluctant monster who blames Christianization for her curse, is compelled to destroy until she is destroyed. The fact that the destructive forces in both worlds, the bride and her mother, are female intensifies the sense of horror in the poem because the typically life-giving woman destroys life in this poem: the bride blames her mother for her death by suicide, which compels her to return as a vampire to kill her lover. This image of the young woman "who dies on the eve of her marriage or reunion with a lover, and then haunts him until she succeeds in luring him into her world of death" is common in folklore throughout Europe and thus an appropriate figure for ballad poetry (Allen 1983, 46). More specifically, as we have seen, it is common in vampire folklore for a person to die before his or her time as a result of violent death such as suicide, murder, or an accident, or from an inexplicable illness, and is doomed to return as a vampire.[25] As a vampire, she ideally represents the monstrous Other as it applies to the youth's fantasies of her as a woman and a Christian, and as it applies to the imposition of one culture on another. As a vampire, she must die if "young folk," representative of modernity, are to live. Similarly, the old religion must die to make way for the more modern religion and culture of Christianity.

Goethe's bride enters the young man's room just as he was falling asleep: "Scarce are closed his eyes" when the woman appears at his door. There is no mention of the youth awakening to someone at his door. This sequence is indicative of the beginnings of a dream which apparently continues for the remainder of the poem and possibly beyond, since there is no indication that the youth awakens and no closure to the ballad. In the original story from antiquity, the youth Machates is not aware of the fact that his bride had died six months earlier. When he is visited by her ghost, he believes it is she. In Goethe's rendition of this story, as well, the youth does not know that his bride is dead. With these fears of the Unknown, of the Other, still fresh on his mind, he begins to fall asleep and his bride appears to him. If we accept that the young man is dreaming of an encounter with his bride, then the vampire in this poem is a direct manifestation of cultural fears and anxieties and, as a monster, the vampire is a cultural body that embodies these fears (Carroll 1990, 207; Cohen 1996, 7). According to Freud, the unconscious is a repository of repressed desires, impulses, and wishes of a sexual and sometimes destructively aggressive nature. He goes on to explain that in sleep one views the unconscious as a landscape "inhabited by those aspects of life that go on living, the realm of the undead spoken through dreams" (quoted in Melton 1999, 492). Also according to Freudian psychoanalysis, "vampire narratives express [. . .] the fascination [. . .] which the living take in death and the dead" (quoted in Melton 1999, 492).

From this perspective—the ballad as the youth's dream—the metaphorical significance of the vampire in literature of the eighteenth and nineteenth centuries becomes more distinct. In his dream and fantasy of this woman he has never met, but has longed for, the young man creates an ambiguous nature for her. She is at the same time his fellow human, but also the Other, something unknown to him because she is female and Christian. Reading the rest of the ballad as a dream in the Freudian sense, the woman in her demure appearance is an object of the young man's fantasy. This virtuous, restrained, innocent, and beautiful, yet simultaneously passionately sexual woman is what he desires to see because he believes he actually will see her. Later in his dream, however, he identifies her with her family's new-found Christianity, which he does not understand and thus fears. She, and thus Christianity, becomes the evil Other—the vampire. According to Freud, "many things which, if they were real, could give no enjoyment, can do so in the play of fantasy" (quoted in Melton 1999, 713). The experience in this ballad would be quite horrible indeed for all involved if it were portrayed as real. It only becomes officially unreal for the reader and those involved in stanza 18, after more than half of the ballad has been read. The reader finds out about this woman's true ambiguous nature as a vampire at approximately the same time the characters find out about her, though Goethe provides several clues beforehand. The horrible events of the poem are masked by the supernatural quality of the ballad because the enlightened reader would have to ascribe a metaphorical significance to the vampire figure. In addition to the supernatural element, the song-like quality of the ballad itself contrasts with and minimizes the horror of the subject matter.

The possibility of the ballad being the youth's dream only intensifies the metaphorical significance of the vampire and of the woman as vampire in the narrative. The woman's ambiguous nature is in the youth's mind only because the woman as a vampire is created in his dream. In his dream, his desire of what he wants her to be—a virtuous and beautiful bride—conflicts with what she really is as far as he knows—a woman he does not yet know and a Christian. These conflicting views of what the woman is converge in his dream with his fears of not being welcomed by the unknown Christians and function as the catalyst for the projection in his dream of the woman as a vampire. By revealing her identity as a vampire in his dream, the youth creates a defense mechanism. If she is a monster, she is no longer human. In the beginning of his dream she was the ideal human woman, but this ideal is as unreal in his fantasy as the portrayal of her as a vampire. His insecurity about being a pagan in a Christian household, and his anxieties about meeting and marrying his bride who is a Christian, cause him to create in his mind an identity for her that becomes ambiguous because he does not know what to expect from her either as a person or as a Christian. The woman in this ballad is perceived to be a vampire by the youth in his dream. He identifies her with Christianity and with the unknown woman. Because of his fears, he creates the ambiguous nature of the Other for her. This Other becomes the evil Other, represented by the vampire figure and her compulsion to kill.

Despite his pioneering efforts in the development of the female literary vampire with the publication of "The Bride of Corinth" and the resulting erotic terror that would become a common characteristic of the literary vampire in the nineteenth century, toward the end of his life Goethe became quite critical of the popularity of the vampire that seemed to be particularly appealing to German Romantic poets in the early part of the nineteenth century. For example, in the first act of *Faust II*, Goethe writes in the scene "Weitläufiger Saal" in stage directions for a herald who introduces groups of guests to a masquerade ball:

> Die Nacht- und Grabdichter lassen sich entschuldigen, weil sie soeben im interessanten Gespräch mit einem frisch erstandenen Vampyren begriffen seien, woraus eine neue Dichtart sich vielleicht entwickeln könnte; der Herold muß es gelten lassen und ruft indessen die griechische Mythologie hervor, die, selbst in moderner Maske, weder Charakter noch Gefälliges verliert. (1.5299)
> (The night and graveyard poets excuse themselves, because they were just now engaged in an interesting conversation with a newly risen vampire, out of which a new form of literature might develop. The herald has to allow it and

calls forth the Greek mythology, which, even in modern costume, loses nothing with regard to character or appeal. [my translation])

The night and graveyard poets to whom Goethe refers are John Polidori, E. T. A. Hoffmann, and Prosper Mérimée. For Goethe, this new trend of vampire fiction is easily superseded by the more reliable and respectable classical mythology that has constant appeal, no matter when it appears on the scene. Clearly, Goethe was not pleased with the popularity of the vampire among respected poets and an educated readership. But it is very likely that he was not only reacting to Polidori, Hoffmann, and Mérimée. There was a lot of vampire activity going on in the theater in the early part of the nineteenth century, and as theater director in Weimar (1791–1817), Goethe was certainly well aware of this as well. In order to explain why Goethe was highly critical of this type of horror literature even though he produced one of the most famous vampire poems, it is important to consider the significance of the philosophical landscape toward the end of the eighteenth century.

Goethe is able to produce an experience of the sublime as it relates to horror literature in "The Bride of Corinth" by thematizing the Kantian distinction between the beautiful and the sublime as it is expressed in Kant's *Critique of Judgment*. According to Kant, the beautiful arises from the contemplation of the completeness and unity of closed forms. In contrast, the sublime arises from the contemplation of objects that make us aware of limitlessness (Heller 1987, 202). Goethe's vampire poem is beautiful in the Kantian sense, because the reader can "contemplate the completeness and unity of closed forms" in the structure, the poetic form, and the language of this poem. In his careful attention to rhyme and meter, balance of dialogue between the youth and the bride, and balance and unity in the plot development of this ballad, Goethe achieves a beautiful poetic form. In the first three stanzas, Goethe sets the scene with an exposition that gives the reader all the relevant information about the youth who travels to Corinth to meet the bride promised to him as a child. He is anxious because he knows that her family has converted to Christianity and his family has not. As he is about to fall asleep, the bride enters his room through the open door. For the next eight stanzas (stanzas 6–13) there is a very balanced dialogue between the two, during which she attempts to retreat and he tries to convince her to stay with him. During this dialogue she attempts to explain to him what has happened, and even gives several clues that she is in fact dead, but he does not comprehend. The middle of the poem (stanza 14) marks the climax of the plot, the *Geisterstunde* (witching hour), midnight, at which point the bride's demeanor changes dramatically. Suddenly she is no longer patient and modest, but instead agitated and passionate: "From his mouth the flame she wildly sips," and "And she comes, and lays her near the boy." The two make passionate love for the next five stanzas (stanzas 16–20) until her mother interrupts them. For the remainder of the poem (stanzas 23–28) the bride explains the curse of her revenant existence to her mother, and blames her for it. The experience of the beautiful in the Kantian sense occurs here primarily from a contemplation of the completeness and unity of closed poetic forms in this well-structured ballad. The experience of the sublime in the Kantian sense arises in the contemplation of objects that make us aware of limitlessness. The sublime is expressed in this poem in the basic "limitlessness" of the vampire and again in the structure of the ballad. In stanza 26, the bride expresses the fundamental limitlessness of her curse to rise from the grave to kill others:

> From my grave to wander I am forc'd,
> Still to seek The Good's long-sever'd link,
> Still to love the bridegroom I have lost,
> And the life-blood of his heart to drink;
> When his race is run,
> I must hasten on,
> And the young must 'neath my vengeance sink.

There is also a sublime limitlessness to the actual story and the ending of the ballad. The ballad closes with the bride's gruesome final plea to her mother in stanza 28 to put an end to her cursed existence by opening her coffin and burning her remains on a funeral pyre:

> "Mother, to this final prayer give ear!
> Let a funeral pile be straightway dress'd;
> Open then my cell so sad and drear,
> That the flames may give the lovers rest!
> When ascends the fire
> From the glowing pyre,
> To the gods of old we'll hasten, blest."

Kant replaces Burke's early description of the sublime as "stillness of astonishment," a quiet sense of awe, with "a mind in motion, specifically between attraction and repulsion" (Heller 1987, 204). Goethe represents this emotion that alternates between attraction and repulsion in his vampire ballad. On the one hand, we are attracted by the beauty of the poetic form of this ballad and the initial idealistic beauty of the bride in her appearance and in her demeanor before the witching hour strikes, only to be repulsed when her true nature bursts forth at the end of the poem in all its wanton passion and brutality. Moreover, with the open ending of the ballad, which leaves her plea to be destroyed unresolved, the reader experiences Gothic dread at the possibility that the limitless terror of this vampire bride is eternal. The effect is one of sublime aesthetic horror.

It seems then, as Heller points out, that Kant laid the foundation for an explanation of the aesthetic pleasures of terror: "The horror thriller and terror fantasy prove to be possible sources of the sublime as Kant formulated it. We can see continuity between Kant's formulations of the experience of the sublime [. . .] and the pleasures of terror fantasy" (Heller 1987, 204). In his third *Critique*, Kant expands on Aristotle's premise in his *Poetics*—that art can certainly portray ugly subjects in a beautiful manner—when he states that "only one type of ugliness cannot be represented according to nature without destroying all aesthetic pleasure and hence aesthetic beauty, namely that which causes disgust" (quoted in Hammermeister 2002, 27). Goethe was disgusted, but in his ballad he had produced the effect of the experience of the sublime. His criticism of the "night and graveyard poets" then is justified, despite his own contribution with his vampire ballad, if it suggests that the "night and graveyard poets" did not achieve an effect of the sublime, as he laments to his friend Zelter: "Das Häßliche, das Abscheuliche, das Nichtswürdige [. . .] ist ihr satanisches Geschäft" (Ugliness, repulsiveness, worthlessness [. . .] is their satanic business).

JOSEPH FREIHERR VON EICHENDORFF: "DAS KALTE LIEBCHEN" ("THE COLD SWEETHEART") AND "DIE SPÄTE HOCHZEIT" ("THE LATE WEDDING")

Joseph Freiherr von Eichendorff wrote two poems that, in contrast to Goethe's ballad, provide no explanation for the identities of the women in his poems as vampires. By the time Eichendorff wrote his vampire poems in 1816 and 1828, readers were very likely so familiar with the vampire from folklore and superstition as well as the literary vampire, popularized by Bürger, Goethe, and contemporary British poets such as John Polidori and Lord Byron, that there was no need for Eichendorff to explain how or why a person might become a vampire. The readers' fascination with the vampire developed more from the suspense created by the interplay of the readers' knowledge of the vampire's identity and the victim's ignorance of what lay ahead.

Though both women in Eichendorff's poems are revenants, only the one in his poem, "The Late Wedding," is also a complete and intentional *femme fatale*—at least in one possible interpretation of her actions. Eichendorff's ballad, "The Cold Sweetheart," is the first known German vampire poem that does not have as its focus the vampiric characteristics or actions of the revenant. Instead, the focus is on the impending tragic consequences for the young man who will join his vampire lover despite her warnings of his likely fate. As we have seen, Goethe's bride in "The Bride of Corinth" goes into great detail when she explains her vampiric nature and preferred manner of death to her mother, albeit not until the end of the poem. By the time Eichendorff wrote "The Cold Sweetheart" in 1816, the motif of the revenant lover who later reveals his or her vampiric nature had already been popular for some time. For this reason, it was not necessary for Eichendorff to dwell on the details of his character's vampire nature, nor is it necessary to address how she became a vampire. It was enough for him to imply her vampiric nature by references, such as her "Kämmerlein" (little room) and how cold it is where she lies: "Hier wird's noch viel kühler sein" (Here it will be much cooler) (l.8) and especially that her lover must follow her to the grave: "Mit ins Grab hinunter muß" (Will have to join me in the grave) (l.16).

In "The Cold Sweetheart," the man ignores repeated requests by the woman to stay away. The woman gives him several vague indications that she is in fact dead and lying in her coffin, but he is determined to lie down with her. Finally, when the witching hour is upon them ("Sieh! Die Sterne schon erblassen" [See! The stars are already fading"; 1.9]), she feels herself falling into an altered state, a "slumber" (l.10). The young man tries to embrace her and suffers from her kiss: "Wahnsinn bringt der Toten Kuß" (The kiss of the dead brings insanity; l.14). In the end she informs him that he must follow her to her grave: "Mit ins Grab hinunter muß" (Will have to join me in the grave). In this poem the woman is an incomplete *femme fatale*, much like Goethe's bride in "The Bride of Corinth," because she resists his advances indirectly by referring to the discomfort of and limited space in her "bed" (stanza 1):

He. Let me in, my sweet darling!

She. My little room is dark.

He. Oh, I'll find a little space.

She. And my bed is small and narrow.

Eichendorff's later vampire poem, "The Late Wedding," begins with a young man's arrival at night for his wedding at his bride's castle. As he approaches the castle, the door opens and he sees his bride seated in a hall on a throne made of diamonds. Her jewels cast a reddish glow throughout the hall, and he sees very silent and pale guests standing in the hall: "Blass' Knaben warten schweigend auf, / Still' Gäste stehn herum" (Pale youths wait silently / Quiet guests stand around; 1.9–10). Slowly, the bride stands up "so hoch und bleich und stumm" (so tall and pale and still). These references to quiet and pale complexions create a nightmarish atmosphere, indicating that this is a wedding party for the dead. The first verse of the poem, "Der Mond ging unter—jetzt ist's Zeit" (The moon set—now it's time) allows for the possibility that this event is repeated nightly at the same hour. This implies that the two lovers may have died before they could marry, and were cursed to repeat this unfulfilled attempt to marry in the afterlife. If this is the case, the groom is part of the dead company in the hall (Haller 1962, 48). On the other hand, only the guests and the bride are described as being silent and pale, namely dead, but the young man is not. Hence, he is more likely to be the only living person in this gathering.

As the bride throws back her golden robes, the young groom shudders with desire: "Da schauert ihn vor Lust" (He shuddered with lust; 1.14). The poem climaxes in the final two verses when the bride reaches out with a cold, white hand and tears the groom's heart from his breast: "Sie langt mit kalter, weißer Hand / Das Herz ihm aus der Brust" (With a cold, white hand she took / his heart from his breast). If we accept that she is tearing out the young man's heart, the bride is clearly a prime example of the complete and truly monstrous *femme fatale*. She is malicious and willful in the groom's destruction. Conversely, these final two lines of the poem may also be understood to imply that she is offering the groom her heart, which she has torn from her own breast. In any case, the final act is horrific, and the ambiguity of the final two lines of the poem only adds to the overall surreal atmosphere of the poem (Haller 1962, 48). The larger metaphoric significance of this violent act is that she destroys his emotions, his love, his passion, and the essence of what makes him human in the Romantic context of this poem when she tears out his heart from his breast. The ambiguous nature of this act creates an atmosphere of horror because it combines fear with revulsion and uncertainty, an important element of horror literature (Carroll 1990, 22). In addition to this, the combined traits of this woman as a seductress, an object of desire for the groom, and a vicious killer make her an extremely palpable example of the vampire *femme fatale* with necrophilic undertones.

Neither the man nor the woman responds to what the other person is saying after the first stanza; they simply speak in turn but do not converse with one another in a meaningful manner. In stark contrast to the enlightened dialogue between Lenore and her mother in Bürger's "Lenore," Eichendorff's "The Cold Sweetheart," consists entirely of a dialogue between two lovers, known to the reader only as Er (He) and Sie (She), that offers no real communication between the two. In fact, the dialogue between the two is mostly derailed or empty, that is, the participants in the dialogue speak alternately, but dialogue partner A does not always address comments made by dialogue partner B when he or she speaks, resulting in an uncanny and unnatural atmosphere in the poem. The entire poem consists of incidents of derailed dialogue, beginning quite effectively with the first stanza:

He. Let me in, my sweet darling!

She. My little room is dark.

He. Oh, I'll find a little space.

She. And my bed is small and narrow.

Her response to his request to join her is that her "little room" is dark. She does not actually respond to his request directly, but instead attempts to make his desire to join her seem undesirable by emphasizing a negative aspect of her "little room," namely that it is dark and dreary. Instead of telling him directly that he should not join her, she circumvents such a confrontation in a passive manner by presenting his desire to join her in a negative light. Her hope is to cause him to take action and decide to not join her in her coffin, through her negative portrayal of the space she has in her "little room." His response to her comment that her "little room" is dark and dreary is that he will find some space. Other than the implication that the space is small, apparent in the word "Kämmerlein" in line 2, space or the lack of space was not the information she intended to convey. The word "finster" (dark) is in the first position in her comment in line 2, which gives it emphasis. In the final line of the stanza, however, she picks up on his remark regarding space by mentioning that her bed is narrow and small. Eichendorff's use of the conjunction "und" (and) to begin her remark suggests that she is continuing her comment from line 2 at the end of the stanza. This pattern of derailed dialogue continues throughout the poem and, combined with her attempts to keep him from joining her, leads to noncommunication between the two and his ultimate death.

The cross-rhyme of the four-line stanzas, however, binds the two in this apparent noncommunicative dialogue. In the abab rhyme scheme, the young man is always "a" and she is "b." The cross-rhyme links each of their own statements, and thus emphasizes the overlapping nature of their dialogue. The rhyme scheme connects each dialogue partner to what he or she said previously, but the two still remain detached from one another. For example, his comments in lines 1 and 3 of stanza 1 are connected to one another through the rhyme, as are her comments in lines 2 and 4, but "He" and "She" as dialogue partners remain unconnected.

He. Let me in, my sweet darling! (a)

She. My little room is dark. (b)

He. Oh, I'll find a little space. (a)

She. And my bed is small and narrow. (b)

While dialogue is at least implied in "The Cold Sweetheart," especially in the dramatic structure of the poem with alternating lines spoken by Er and Sie, in the ballad "The Late Wedding" there is absolutely no verbal communication between the groom and his intended bride, or with anyone else in the hall for that matter. The bride and the groom communicate with one another only through gestures. In this ballad there is a threefold reference to the silence among the company gathered in the hall in the first four lines of the second stanza: "Pale youths wait *silently* / *Quiet* guests stand around, / Then the bride rose slowly, / So tall and pale and *still*" (my emphasis). Precisely this unnatural and solemn quiet among the wedding guests in the dazzling hall communicates enough about this uncanny scene, rendering verbal communication unnecessary. The groom has joined the (un)dead in this hall, and in order to communicate what she must, the bride need only make three distinct gestures: she rises slowly from her throne, casts back her golden robes, and tears the groom's heart from his breast in one violent motion.

In lieu of verbal communication between the bride and the groom, the gestures they make give the reader some insight into the nature of their relationship. As he enters the hall he sees her seated on her throne of diamonds, and her jewels cast a red glow throughout the hall. As he approaches her his reaction is one of desire, apparent anticipation, and some fear: "Da schauert ihn vor Lust" (He shuddered with lust). He is not terrified at this point, but rather seems to be strangely excited. Her height as she rises from her throne is remarkable: "Then the bride rose slowly, / So tall and pale and still" and very likely signifies more than just her physical stature. It may in fact imply that her social status is higher than his, or that she is in some other way dominant. Whether this is true or not, this bride is clearly larger than life from the groom's perspective, as he looks up at her from his position at the base of her throne. Although he has come to her castle to marry her, the silence between the two and the fact that she rises "so hoch" (so tall) from her throne as he approaches suggests that she is simply acknowledging the presence of a visitor, not welcoming her fiancé; there is no apparent familiarity that one would expect to find between two people who are about to be married.

Whereas the vampire in Goethe's ballad appears in a religious context, Eichendorff uses the vampire in "The Late Wedding" for a different type of social commentary. Eichendorff's vampire bride is one of the first known aristocratic vampires in German literature.[26] In her dual nature as a powerful member of this social hierarchy and as a vampire, the bride in Eichendorff's poem represents an (un)dead social class; outwardly aristocracy seems to be alive, awesome, and even immensely powerful, but it is in fact nothing more than a shell, an ancient construct that has lost its spirit, its raison d'être—a reanimated corpse. In contrast to the newly developing application of the vampire as a metaphor for the predatory nature of capitalism and aristocracy in the nineteenth century,[27] Eichendorff, whose family belonged to the landed gentry, mourns the slow death of his own social class in this poem. Even though the bride is violent in the end, up until she tears the groom's heart from his breast, the image Eichendorff gives of the wedding party in the hall is reminiscent of a wake. As a representative of aristocracy, she arrogantly destroys her class's future by not condescending to marriage, in other words, cooperating with the lesser nobility, as represented by her suitor.[28] The bride also does not *prey* on the lower social classes in this poem, as do Marx's metaphorical vampires and Stoker's vampire at the end of the nineteenth century, but rather she *destroys* an apparently lower-ranking member of her own social class, whom she had planned to marry. This seems to reflect Eichendorff's own internal struggle with a changing society, in which aristocracy had no future. Eichendorff was also frustrated by the growing divide between the landed gentry that was becoming impoverished, and the higher nobility that was passing on capital to the bourgeoisie with its extravagance and excess (Hillach and Krabiel 1972, 6).

In literature, a castle is a motif if it performs certain functions that move the plot along instead of being used as a mere setting. These functions include: 1) providing a luxurious setting that symbolizes materialistic indulgence; 2) creating an atmosphere of horror by introducing ghosts and other unexplainable phenomena that instill a sense of mortal fear; and 3) representing a place of political and social authority that either attracts or repels people, depending on the poet's intention (Daemmerich and Daemmerich 1987, 57). Eichendorff combines all three of these functions of the castle motif in "The Late Wedding." In conjunction with the vampire theme of this poem, the castle, everything that it represents, and everyone associated with it is dead, dying, or doomed. As a motif within a ballad with a vampire theme, the castle functions here as the vampire's home, and as such is immediately associated with death. In fact, it functions as a large tomb. Moreover, in conjunction with the *femme fatale* motif, the castle as a motif often functions as a "pleasure palace," which in turn is often linked with the motif of "dodging one's duty" (Daemmrich and Daemmrich 1987, 104).

In Eichendorff's poetry, enclosed spaces, whether they are rooms, buildings, or even enclosed spaces in forests and valleys such as ravines, are associated with threatening events and feelings of anxiety. Moreover, the people in Eichendorff's poetry who demonstrate discomfort or feelings of anxiety in enclosed spaces are presented in a sympathetic manner (Hillach and Krabiel 1972, 243). By the same token, those who feel comfortable in enclosed spaces, rather than in open surroundings in nature, are portrayed in a more negative light, often as the "Philister" (philistines) much despised by Eichendorff (Hillach and Krabiel 1972, 243). These feelings of entrapment in enclosed spaces that are typically associated with bourgeois contentment are evident in Eichendorff's vampire poems as well.

In "The Late Wedding," the hall of the bride's castle is an enclosed and horrifying space that houses a vampire bride, and though it is much larger than the coffin in "The Cold Sweetheart," it is nonetheless a tomb. On the one hand the hall in this castle, with all its glory and riches, represents the highest aristocracy, but at the same time it houses a dead company. When the groom enters the hall and sees his bride sitting on a throne of diamonds, he is bedazzled by her riches. The first impression that the groom, and through his narrated perspective, the reader, has of the castle is one of luxury and materialistic indulgence—a common symbolic treatment of castles and one of the primary functions of the motif. Immediately following this image of extreme wealth, Eichendorff creates an atmosphere of supernatural horror in his description of the silent and pale wedding guests, the servants, and the bride herself. This image of the castle that houses supernatural phenomena, such as ghosts or vampires, is the second function of the castle motif, namely one that instills mortal fear through its supernatural inhabitants.

Before his death, however, there is a brief but significant reference to the groom's state of mind after he has seen the "pale" guests and his bride. He does not seem to be in fear of his life as one might expect during this eerie encounter. Instead, in a truly Romantic sense of love in death or love of death, which connects this modern poem with the necrophilia taboo that is common to German vampire folklore,[29] the groom shudders with desire or lust for his (un)dead bride. The third function of the castle motif is that it represents a place of political and social authority that can attract or repel people. The association of the castle as the center of political authority is as common as its association with excessive wealth. It may in fact be enough to say that the castle as a motif represents political and financial power. In this poem, the castle as a place of political authority attracts the groom, but also repels him. He is stunned by the wealth he sees in the hall, but he *shudders* with lust nonetheless. If we remember that there is some indication in Eichendorff's poem that the bride may be from a higher social class than the groom and somehow unattainable for him despite the planned wedding, the juxtaposition of the vampire theme with the location in the hall of a castle stands for a "living dead" social class—the aristocracy. The lower aristocracy, represented here by the groom, is bedazzled by the wealth and apparent splendor of the (dead) aristocracy and lusts after its privileges. In so doing, it loses heart, succumbs to temptation, and becomes subservient to the (dead) aristocracy.

EROTICISM, DEATH, AND THE VAMPIRE

In the first vampire poems, German poets effectively combined the universal themes of death, love, lost or denied love, and grief with the vampire theme and related motifs to create a personification of eroticized death that functioned as a template for a variety of cultural fears and anxieties, including war (Ossenfelder, Bürger), religious anxieties (Ossenfelder, Bürger, Goethe), life or love in death (Bürger, Goethe, Eichendorff), and class anxieties

(Goethe, Eichendorff). In literature, death occurs both as a theme and as a motif. Many of these motifs occur in conjunction with death or the associated motif, "dead lover returns." These include, but are not limited to, the dance of death, images of the Grim Reaper, sleep, and darkness (Daemmrich and Daemmrich 1987, 78). Because death is the negation of life, in literature it is often associated with an evaluation of life. Death is often a welcome release from a dreadful or painful life; conversely, if life on earth is desirable and highly valued, then death is generally feared. Literary works from the Middle Ages, the Reformation, and the Baroque and Romantic eras, for example, portray death as a release from the superficiality of worldly power and possessions and promise everlasting life after death for the faithful (Caswell and Goodwin 1988, 328; Daemmrich and Daemmrich 1987, 79). Though death is often portrayed as a release from a painful life, it is nevertheless feared. Especially in late medieval and Baroque literature, the motif of the dance of death, usually performed by one or more hideous skeletons, was intended to remind readers that all people will die, regardless of their social status in life. In the nineteenth century, German Romantic poets expressed the complex emotions involved in the contemplation of death that ranged from fear to joy, and from grief over the death of a loved one to a desire to join that person in death.

In conjunction with the vampire theme, death in the poems discussed here is not only something to be feared, but *someone* to be feared—someone familiar. More than that, the vampire, Death, is intimately familiar with his or her victim. This intimate connection to Death is intensified in the eroticization of death in the guise of the vampire as the dead lover who returns. This contrasts with the very unerotic vampires from central European folklore, but it connects the German literary vampire to the necrophilia theme that is common to German vampire folklore. Although the vampire from folklore and superstition did not always kill his victims, he was familiar to the victim as a member of the victim's immediate family or community, and in the case of German vampire folklore in particular, the revenant was often the victim's lover. German poets combined characteristics of the central European vampire superstition with characteristics of German vampire folklore to create a new monster that eroticized death. In Ossenfelder's poem, the vampire's love for the young woman apparently had not been reciprocated. He returns to take revenge on his dear "Christianchen" because she will not return his affections.

Bürger's vampire, Wilhelm, returns for his fiancée because her excessive grief over his death and her rejection of her faith in God do not allow him to rest in his grave. Goethe's bride explains in detail that she is compelled to return from the grave for her pagan lover because of the Christian sin of committing suicide in response to forced conversion to Christianity. Eichendorff's vampires are both women who kill their lovers, though they differ greatly in their demeanors and their intentions. In "The Cold Sweetheart," the vampire warns her lover several times, but is ultimately compelled to kill him because of his love in death when he expresses his desire to lie with her corpse. In Eichendorff's later poem, "The Late Wedding," however, the vampire is more deliberate and aggressive in her representation of an admired yet "dead" social hierarchy in a time of social and political revolution in the years between the Congress of Vienna (1815) and the March Revolution (1848). The attribute of "erotic death" that is evident in the earliest literary vampires prevails today and is commonly associated with the vampires of nineteenth-century British poets, such as Lord Byron, Sheridan Le Fanu, and Bram Stoker, to name a few.[30] It is important to remember, however, that this concept of eroticized Death in the guise of the vampire pre-dated Romanticism in the earliest vampire poems by German poets.

The dream motif that occurs in the first three German vampire poems by Ossenfelder, Bürger, and Goethe with varying degrees of conspicuousness is particularly important, because it is the one motif besides "dead lover returns" that is also represented in the original folklore. Though the appearance of the vampire and its subsequent destruction may vary slightly from one report or folk story to the next, two things remain constant: the vampire is a loved one who has returned from the grave, and he or (less frequently) she returns while the victim sleeps. Most accounts of torment by a vampire in the reports collected for Charles VI include very detailed and vivid dreams of the vampire smothering the victim in his or her sleep.

In addition to establishing this direct link to the original folklore, and probably of far greater interest to the poets who used it in their poetry, the introduction of a dream, or even its mere suggestion, is a useful technique to increase the suspense in a narrative (Daemmrich and Daemmrich 1987, 94). Especially when one considers the general vampire theme in these poems, the mere hint that the victim may in fact be dreaming of the encounter with his or her vampire lover can have a wide range of uses for the poet. The unimaginable horror of encountering a vampire in the guise of a lover becomes a very routine rendezvous between lovers when it happens in a dream. In addition to this, the vampire as a figure in the victim's dream may imply that the victim has a subconscious fear of this person or of what the person represents. The dream motif is also commonly used as a metaphor for the transience of life (Weidhorn 1988, 407). The evidence of a dream in which the vampire figures prominently enhances the element of the fantastic surrounding the vampire figure, which is ultimately the only conceivable receptacle for this figure of superstition in the enlightened West.

Each of the poems by Ossenfelder, Bürger, and Goethe uses the dream motif in conjunction with the vampire theme for a different reason or set of reasons. Ossenfelder uses the dream to show how the vampire will approach his beloved. The poems by Bürger and Goethe use the vampire theme in conjunction with the dream motif to build the suspense of the narrative and to add a feeling of vagueness to the narrative. Much as the vampire's identity is gradually revealed in these poems, so is the dream merely implied rather than blatantly stated, as it is in Ossenfelder's poem. This adds to the general feeling of suspense and uncertainty in the poems. In addition to establishing a connection to the folklore, the vampire's attack during his or her victim's sleep delivers a safe space for the expression of the implied victim's fears and anxieties. In this application, the vampire is truly a cultural body upon which we project our fears (Cohen 1996, 7). While Ossenfelder's poem addresses the folkloric connection between the vampire and the dream, Bürger's and Goethe's poems use the dream as a literary technique that increases suspense and sets the mood, while simultaneously providing a venue for the metaphorical signification of the vampire.

Modern readers have become accustomed to the numerous Christian symbols that occur in vampire literature and film. These include the Christian cross or crucifix, holy water, and sometimes the consecrated host, not to mention the mere faith of clergy. In fact, these symbols, which had long been used to ward off evil in general, were being applied by nineteenth-century authors as a weapon against the new representative of supernatural evil, the vampire. In contrast to later vampire literature from the nineteenth century, the first vampire poems by German poets do not provide any insight into the means by which one can prevent an attack by a vampire, very likely because prevention from attack was not the focus of the folklore. The vampire phenomenon was new to western Europe, and the only reported methods that can be considered preventative of further vampire attacks were the proper destruction and disposal of the vampire's body. This is reflected in the folklore and in reports from which the poets very likely gathered their information on the vampire. The folklore and the reports by scientists primarily offered information on people who can possibly become a vampire, how and when vampires attack, how they appear when their bodies are exhumed, and how they can ultimately be destroyed. There is no information on preventing vampire attacks in the reports written for Charles VI, because enlightened scientists were more interested in studying the phenomenon using scientific methods than they were in addressing preventative techniques. After all, discussion of protection against vampires is an acceptance of their existence, and this is something enlightened scientists were not willing to do.

The numerous methods that we accept today as vampire repellents, such as garlic, the crucifix, and holy water, for example, already existed as methods for warding off evil in general and included the vampire because of its evil nature and thus its association with the devil. In literature, the use of these and other items to protect against vampire attacks was not taken up by the German poets, but instead by the British poets of the nineteenth century. The early German vampire poetry reflects the initial stages of knowledge of the vampire in Europe. The conscious act of preventing an attack by a vampire logically implies a pre-existing knowledge of and belief in vampires. For this reason, it became more important in the later nineteenth century to have knowledge of useful preventative measures, since the literary vampire as an entity was already commonplace in poetry, prose, and drama. This progression of awareness of the vampire phenomenon culminated at the end of the nineteenth century in Bram Stoker's *Dracula*, which features a scholar, Van Helsing, who studies and hunts vampires as part of his profession. This innovation is particularly interesting to a readership that had become familiar with the vampire and the prevention of attacks. This pre-existing knowledge paves the way for a new and very modern literary innovation that has defined much of the vampire literature and film that followed in the twentieth century: the vampire hunter.

NOTES

The poems discussed in this chapter are reproduced in English translation in the appendix.

1. See chapter 3.
2. Anacreontic poetry was written in the style of the Greek lyric poet Anacreon, who died in 478 BC. The tone of this style of poetry is very life-affirming and festive. Typical themes include wine, friendship, and sexual love.
3. Tokaj is the correct spelling for this town in German and Hungarian. Though the word "Tockayer" is the correct term for the wine of the region, it is also likely from the context of this statement by the poem's narrator that the poet intended to refer to the town when he wrote, "And *in* Tockay today / Will drink you into a vampire" ("Ich will dich *in* Tockayer / Zu einem Vampir trinken") (my emphasis). It is very likely that Ossenfelder either confused the name of the town with the name of the popular wine or that he intentionally used the name of the wine to refer to the town, because the wine from this region was popular in Germany and wine is also a common element of anacreontic poetry ("Tokaj" and "Tokajer"; interview with Frank Baron, professor of German at the University of Kansas and a native Hungarian).
4. See chapter 3 for further discussion of Flückinger's report.
5. "Tisa" is the Serbian spelling for the river Tisza.
6. Specifically, he says: "As people along the Theyse / Believe staunchly and *heyduck-like* / In vampires that bring death." ("Als Völker an der Theyse / An tödtliche Vampire / *Heyduckisch* feste glauben) (my emphasis). Johann Christoph Adelung explains the term "heyduck" in his dictionary, *Grammatisch-kritisches Wörterbuch der Hochdeutschen Mundart* (Grammatical Critical Dictionary of the High German Dialect;1796, 1067) as follows: "Der Heiduck . . . , ein Ungarisches Wort, welches eigentlich einen leicht gewaffneten Soldaten zu Fuß bedeutet. In Deutschland beleget man mit diesem Nahmen einen Diener in der Tracht dieser Ungarischen Heiducken, dessen vornehmstes Amt darin bestehet, die Kutsche oder Sänfte seines Herren zu begleiten" ("The Heyduck . . . , a Hungarian word, which actually signifies a lightly armed foot soldier. In Germany this name is used for a servant in the traditional dress of the Hungarian heyduck, whose most refined duty consists of accompanying his master's carriage or sedan-chair" [my translation]). Ossenfelder's use of the word *heyduckisch* (heyduck-like) in this poem, then, has a dual purpose: it draws the connection between Germany and Hungary and associates superstition with the lower classes.
7. This name, Christiane, is the feminine equivalent of the masculine name Christian in German. The translation I have come across for this poem, however, erroneously uses the word "Christian." I have replaced it with a reasonable translation of the name as "Christiana" to avoid the confusion that results from the use of the word "Christian" in the existing translation cited in Melton (1999, 470).

8. See chapter 3.

9. In these excerpts from Scott's translation, I have used his numbers for the stanzas. Because Scott structurally altered the stanzas, these numbers do not correspond with Bürger's stanzas.

10. Scott's translated verses were collected from his memoirs, *The Poetical Works of Sir Walter Scott, with Memoir of the Author*, vol. 6, 156–70.

11. The Seven Years' War was the last of three Silesian wars waged between Prussia and the Austro-Hungarian Empire from about 1740 to 1763. As a result of his victories in these wars, King Frederick II (Frederick the Great) was able to gain lands in central Europe, primarily Silesia and Bohemia, that turned Prussia into a European superpower and started the historic rivalry between Prussia and Austria (Koepke 2000, 88).

12. Though there are numerous examples of animals in classical Greek and Roman mythology, one example is Jupiter's transformation into an eagle, a swan, and a bull in Ovid's *Metamorphosis* in order to seduce humans. For the purposes of the discussion in this chapter, it is important to recall the Greek empusae, incubae, and the children of Hecate, who were female vampire-like demons that were apparently brought from Palestine to Greek mythology. In Palestine they belonged to the Lilim, which means "children of Lilith." In Greek mythology they sucked the blood from young men in an effort to steal their vitality. In this mythology, they appeared variably as donkeys, female dogs, or as beautiful young women—the most common disguise used to seduce young men. Their donkey-like traits in particular had the function of emphasizing their most defining character traits—lechery and cruelty (Graves 1960, 189–90).

13. One example from modern German literature that immediately comes to mind is Gregor's willing transformation in Franz Kafka's *Metamorphosis* (1915) in an effort to retreat from his dreaded human existence and responsibilities.

14. Examples of the horse representing the rider's inner demon or struggle for self-realization, i.e., the struggle to understand one's own nature, is featured in Goethe's poem, "An Schwager Kronos" (1774); his drama, *Egmont* (1787); in Theodor Storm's novella, *Der Schimmelreiter*, and in Franz Kafka's story, "Ein Landarzt," to cite a few examples.

15. This observation was made by Jonathan Harker in chapter 3 of *Dracula*: "But my very feelings changed to repulsion and terror when I saw the whole man [Count Dracula] slowly emerge from the window and begin to crawl down the castle wall over that dreadful abyss, *face down*, with his cloak spreading out around him like great wings . . . just as a lizard moves along a wall" (Stoker 1993, 49; Stoker's emphasis).

16. This is an observation by Jonathan Harker in chapter 1: "As he [the driver/Count Dracula] swept his long arms . . . as though brushing aside some impalpable obstacle, the wolves fell back further still" (Stoker 1993, 23). Dracula also solicits the help of a wolf from a zoo near Lucy Westenra's home. The wolf breaks a window in her home to allow Dracula entry (177–82).

17. Dracula transforms into a bat that flaps its wings against Lucy Westenra's windows before each of his attacks on her. Eventually Lucy becomes accustomed to this repeated nuisance. An example from Lucy's journal in chapter 11: "I went to the window and looked out, but could see nothing, except a big bat, which had evidently been buffeting its wings against the window" (Stoker 1993, 185). Dracula jumps from his ship, the *Demeter*, in the shape of a dog upon his arrival in England. This is first noted in chapter 7 in a newspaper clipping: "The very instant the shore was touched, an immense dog sprang up on deck from below . . . and, running forward, jumped from the bow on the sand" (105).

18. This characteristic of the vampire, i.e., that he may not enter a dwelling uninvited, was applied later by Samuel Taylor Coleridge in his poem, "Christabel" (1798), and by Bram Stoker in *Dracula*.

19. See Paul Barber's book *Vampires, Burial, and Death: Folklore and Reality* for more on the stories "The Shoemaker from Silesia," "Peter Plogojowitz," and "Vrykolakas."

20. According to his friend Friedrich von Müller, Goethe actually denied that this story by Phlegon of Tralles was his source for the ballad. He gave no indication of any other sources, and only mentioned that the bride's name was Philinnion, which is the young woman's name in

the original story from antiquity. See Ernst Beutler (ed.), *Gedenkausgabe der Werke, Briefe und Gespräche*, vol. 23, 348.

21. All quotes from Goethe's poem, "The Bride of Corinth," are from Trunz.

22. Leavy reserves the term *belle dame sans merci* for the immortal fatal woman, and the term *femme fatale* for the mortal fatal woman (169).

23. When Goethe wrote this ballad in 1797, the only earlier vampire figures in German literature were the unnamed male vampire in the first German vampire poem, Ossenfelder's "Der Vampir," and Wilhelm in Bürger's ballad, "Lenore." Both of these vampire figures were male and were more obviously malicious and monstrous than the bride in Goethe's ballad. It is important to note here as well that the British tradition of the literary vampire that would become increasingly popular and influential in the nineteenth century had not yet begun in 1797. One year later, in 1798, Samuel Taylor Coleridge introduced the vampire into British literature with his poem, "Christabel."

24. For example, Sheridan Le Fanu's female vampire in *Carmilla* (1872) is a rather ruthless, manipulative, and deceitful character who shares these qualities with Coleridge's female vampire, Geraldine, from his poem, "Christabel" (1798). Bram Stoker carried on this tradition of the truly monstrous female vampire when Lucy Westenra was turned into a vampire in his novel, *Dracula* (1897), and fed on children in a manner that is reminiscent of the Greek lamia.

25. See chapter 1 for causes of vampirism in central European vampire folklore and superstition.

26. Technically, Samuel Taylor Coleridge introduced the first aristocratic vampire to poetry in his ballad, "Christabel" (1798). Like Bürger and Goethe before him, however, Coleridge does not mention vampires specifically in his poem and, unlike Goethe, Coleridge did not identify Geraldine outright as a vampire. It is generally agreed, however, that the aristocratic Lady Geraldine is a vampire, due to the many vampire traits that she exhibits (Melton 1999, 108–9).

27. Specifically, Karl Marx and Bram Stoker apply the image of the vampire as a metaphor to demonstrate how capitalism and aristocracy, respectively, feed viciously off the lower social classes, effectively draining their life force. Marx believed that there was a basic metaphorical vampiric relationship between capital and labor, for example. In chapter 10 of the first volume of *Capital,* originally published in 1867, Marx writes that "capital is dead labour, that, vampire-like, only lives by sucking living labour, and lives the more, the more labour it sucks" (Marx 1999, 149). In this statement, Marx uses the metaphor of the vampire to contrast living labor, namely the working class, with dead labor, raw materials and machinery (Melton 1999, 482).

28. It is very likely that the bridegroom is of a lower rank in the social hierarchy because he looks up at her as she rises from her throne: "Then the bride rose slowly, / So tall and pale and still."

29. See chapter 1.

30. In 1813, Lord Byron wrote a vampire poem, "The Giaour," which was the only overt occurrence of the vampire in his work. In the spring of 1816, Lord Byron and his doctor, John Polidori, went to Lake Geneva and stayed in a villa with Percy Bysshe Shelley and Mary Godwin. On June 15, the weather was so bad that Lord Byron suggested they stay indoors and write ghost stories. The most productive literary endeavor that evening was Mary Godwin's story, "Frankenstein," which was later expanded to a novel. John Polidori kept notes on Lord Byron's story, which told of two friends who traveled to the continent, much like he and Polidori had done. One of the friends died, but made the other man promise to keep his death a secret. The second man returned to England only to find that the first man had beaten him back and had begun an affair with the second man's sister. John Polidori published this story in 1819, though it was initially attributed to Lord Byron. Polidori's story became the first treatment of the vampire figure in prose fiction (Melton 1999, 71). In 1872, Sheridan Le Fanu published a collection of stories, *In a Glass Darkly*, that included the novella *Carmilla*, widely regarded as one of the best vampire stories. Bram Stoker read it before he published his famous novel, *Dracula*, in 1897.

Chapter Three

The First German Vampire Stories

All that we see or seem is but a dream within a dream.—Edgar Allan Poe, "A Dream within a Dream"

Following on the coattails of the poets who came before them, German authors Ludwig Tieck (1773–1853), E. T. A. Hoffmann (1776–1822), Ernst Benjamin Salomo Raupach (1784–1852), Theodor Hildebrandt (1794–1859), and Karl Adolf von Wachsmann (1787–1862) reinvented the vampire for prose, becoming trailblazers for vampire fiction since the nineteenth century. Their influence is evident even today in the recent surge of vampire youth romance and film. In their stories, these authors demonstrate the versatility with which the vampire can be adapted for literature. Tieck makes use of the historical connection between magic and vampirism in his story, "Liebeszauber" (Love Magic). Hoffmann makes a direct connection to the vampire stories from central Europe in the discussion that precedes the telling of the story "Vampirismus" in his collection, *Die Serapionsbrüder* (The Serapion-Brethren, 1819–1821), and he connects these images to the cannibalism of Germany's own vampire-like *Nachzehrer*. Raupach, the author of the story, "Laßt die Todten ruhen," which is well known to English-speaking readers in its translation, "Wake Not the Dead," and which has been connected erroneously to Tieck by British and American scholars, connects images of the vampire from central European vampire superstition with images from Germany's Lenore legend. Hildebrandt introduces the female vampire as a child murderess in his novel, predating Bram Stoker's vampire Lucy from his novel, *Dracula*, by approximately seventy years. And Wachsmann connects the vampire with western European imperialism when the vampire's victims travel through Slovenia to close a real estate transaction, predating Bram Stoker's real estate broker, Johnathan Harker, in *Dracula* by fifty years. Each

74   Chapter 3

of these German authors use the vampire as an embodiment of contemporary social anxieties, taboos, and fears that range in severity from adultery, divorce, infanticide, and abuse to necrophilia and cannibalism.

LUDWIG TIECK: "LIEBESZAUBER" (LOVE MAGIC, 1812)

Ludwig Tieck wrote the first known prose work with a vampire theme in 1811 as part of his fairy-tale collection, *Phantasus: Eine Sammlung von Märchen, Schauspielen und Novellen*, which was first published in two volumes in 1812, several years before John Polidori published the first British vampire story, "The Vampyre," in 1819. In 1816 Tieck added a third volume, and in 1828 he published this story unchanged in his collection, *Ludwig Tieck's Schriften*, in which he added volumes four and five of *Phantasus* (Frank 1985, 1295). Tieck had already conceived the idea for this collection of stories during his time in Jena during 1799–1800 where he interacted with August Wilhelm Schlegel, his wife Caroline, Friedrich Schlegel, and his future wife Dorothea Veit. His plan was to model his collection of stories after the gatherings the friends had at the Schlegel household to tell stories and discuss literature, by connecting the individual stories in the collection with critical discussion of the stories and their aesthetic value among the various members of the group. "Love Magic" was one of the new stories that Tieck wrote for this collection. Tieck had been an avid reader since his earliest childhood and was particularly interested in stories of knights, robbers, and horror, no matter how trivial, which had a great impact on his own desire to produce horror and fantasy literature himself (Trainer 1964, 28–29).

"Love Magic" and another story that Tieck included in *Phantasus*, "Der Pokal" (The Trophy; 1811) belong to his *Stadtmärchen* (urban fairy tales), which are also the first urban fairy tales in German literature. The unusual setting for a fairy tale, in the city instead of the countryside, reflects a shift in genre from the common fantastical fairy tale or, more specifically, the *Kunstmärchen* (literary fairy tales) to the more "realistic" novella (Frank 1985, 1297). For Tieck, an important characteristic of the novella that he included in many of his *Phantasus* fairy tales is the common feature of a turning point in the plot that he so admired in the works of Bocaccio, Cervantes, and Goethe. Tieck places the turning point in his "Love Magic" urban fairy tale in the middle of the story when Emil loses consciousness and becomes afflicted with amnesia. This incident marks the end of the first part of the story, which takes place in the city. The catastrophe occurs in Emil's recognition of who his new bride really is, as it does in his other *Phantasus Märchen*, "Der blonde Eckbert" (Fair Eckbert) and "Tannhäuser" (Frank 1985, 1298). Moreover, Tieck applies the motifs from "Fair Eckbert" of marriage to the unrecognized lover, remembrance of repressed memories, insanity, and death to "Love Magic," though the incest motif does not feature in "Love Magic."

The convergence of fantasy as it is represented by the image of the vampire and black magic combined with the real world of a young man in a big city has a greater impact on the reader of "Love Magic" than it would if it were presented in the known fantasy world of the common fairy tale. By placing elements of the supernatural (vampire and black magic) in the mundane life of a typical young man in a big city, Tieck creates the "experience of reality and fantasy as one vision of horror" (Paulin 1985, 199). Tieck formulates his personal views on the literary value of supernatural horror as follows:

> My own view is that the supernatural is a perfectly legitimate subject for imaginative works of art, with the proviso, however, that by his power of suggestion, the author succeeds in subjecting the reader's imagination to his own, in other words, succeeds in lulling the reader's logical faculties and hypnotizing him into the charmed circle of the writer's own imagination. (quoted in Trainer 1964, 69)

As probably one of the most effective horror stories in Tieck's opus, "Love Magic" insists that "a world more terrible than our own imaginings can intervene in our real, everyday life" (Paulin 1985, 199). In this, it functions as a precursor to the horror novellas of E. T. A. Hoffmann (especially "The Sandman") and Edgar Allan Poe.

After one member of the group of friends, Manfred, finishes telling his story, "Rune Mountain," Lothar tells the story, "Love Magic," with the intent of brightening the mood that Manfred's story left among the group. The story begins with the protagonist, Emil, as he waits for his friend, Roderich, to return to their apartment. Emil is a quiet, contemplative, serious, and wealthy young man who has been traveling after the death of his parents. On his travels he had met Roderich, whose carefree, impulsive, and fun-loving temperament is vastly different from his own, and though they often had differing viewpoints, Emil asks Roderich to be his traveling companion. Emil waits for Roderich in great anticipation, because he has something important to tell him. However, it is Carnival time in this city and Roderich is delayed because he has been attending a masquerade ball. The secret that Emil wants to discuss with Roderich involves his infatuation with and love for a young woman he has observed in the house across the street from his apartment. For some time he has watched her play with a little orphan girl she had adopted. Little does he know that the young woman is equally infatuated with Emil, if not more so.

When Roderich does arrive, accompanied by a friend from the ball, Emil is displeased with his friend's tardiness and general frivolity. They argue about Emil's dislike of dancing and music as well as his numerous phobias.

After Roderich leaves, Emil decides to go to the masquerade ball that Roderich had hoped he would attend, because he believes the young woman may be there, since she has not appeared in the window. On his way to the ball, Emil takes a shortcut through the cemetery and is witness to an eerie transaction between an ugly old woman (the witch archetype in fairy tales) and two men. From the men she receives two lamps and expresses very cryptically her greatest concern: "daß sie ganz nach Vorschrift und Kunst gegossen sind, damit die Wirkung nicht ausbleibt" (that they should be formed precisely according to the instructions, so that the effect is maintained) (Frank 1985, 219). Emil hears even more curious details about this odd transaction when one of the men asks the old woman: "Ist es möglich, Alexia, daß dergleichen Zeremonien und Formeln, diese seltsamen alten Sagen [. . .] den freien Willen des Menschen fesseln und Liebe und Haß erregen können?" (Is it possible, Alexia, that these types of ceremonies and formulas, these old legends [. . .] trap people's free will and can stimulate love and hate?) (Frank 1985, 219). She confirms that this is so, but adds that the two people must come together for the effect to be complete; formulas, incantations, and objects, such as the lamps alone, will not suffice. Emil is shaken by what he has witnessed, but after a short prayer to the Virgin Mary, he continues on his way to the ball.

He gets lost in the confusion of the masquerade ball, and although he does not find the young woman, he does find Roderich and his friend from earlier that evening, known here as "the Spaniard" because of his costume. Emil speaks with the Spaniard for a while about Roderich, and then leaves. At home he writes a poem about his experiences at the ball. When he finishes, he notices the young woman in the window of the house across the street and watches her as he has done many times before. This time she places two lamps in the corners of the room and lays a small rug on the table. She leaves the room, and Emil is shocked when he sees the old woman from the cemetery earlier that evening enter the room. When the young woman returns, she is visibly changed: she is noticeably pale, her breasts are bare, and she appears to him to be stiff, "einer Statue von Marmor ähnlich" (like a marble statue) (Frank 1985, 227). Between them the women hold the young girl, who is crying and desperately trying to get the attention of the young woman. But the young woman looks straight ahead, holding the child by the hair in one hand and a silver bowl in the other. Emil witnesses how the old woman speaks some words, and then slits the throat of the little girl. From behind them, what appears to be the head of a dragon rises up and licks the blood from the girl's neck. As the light from the dragon's green eye meets Emil's, he loses consciousness.

The first part of Tieck's story ends here and the second part begins four months later, in the country, on the day of Emil's wedding to the young woman. Through the conversations of Emil's friends at the wedding, the reader learns that Emil had apparently suffered a nervous breakdown that fateful night and as a result he suffered from amnesia. They speak about the unusual encounter Emil had in a park after recovering from his illness at his uncle's house. In this park, his eye caught the eye of a young woman, and he immediately went to her and almost had another nervous breakdown, due to his overwhelming emotions at seeing her. Shortly after this encounter, he asked for her hand in marriage. Her actual identity as the woman Emil had admired from across the street before his nervous breakdown and resulting amnesia is confirmed later by Roderich when he remarks to a wedding guest that the bride seems melancholy because the orphan girl she had cared for had disappeared. As the bride passes among the guests before the wedding, an officer makes comments about her appearance in a way that is already suggestive of a vampire: "Selbst ihre Blässe [. . .] erhöht ihre Schönheit; die braunen Augen blitzen über den bleichen Wangen und unter den dunkeln Haaren so mächtiger hervor, und diese wunderbare, fast brennende Röte der Lippen macht ihr Angesicht zu einem wahrhaft zauberischen Bilde" (Even her pallor [. . .] increases her beauty; her brown eyes shine so powerfully above the pale cheeks and under the dark hair, and that wonderful, almost burning redness of her lips turn her face into a truly magical image) (Frank 1985, 231).

During these preparations, however, Emil is nervous and concerned about something he overheard in the garden earlier that morning. He consults with Roderich and tells him that he saw his bride speaking in confidence with someone who was telling her to be happy, now that she has gotten what she longed for. Roderich is not concerned by this, assuring Emil that it is good that she apparently had been interested in him for some time. In an effort to distract Emil from his brooding, Roderich takes him into the village to witness a wedding between two very poor people. Emil is dismayed when he hears of their bitter poverty, and gives them money. When he finally returns from his despair over the poverty of these people, he and his bride are married. During the dinner following the wedding ceremony, Emil demands that the servants bring wine and food to the poor married couple in the village, so that they may also enjoy their wedding day. He is further disturbed when he sees an ugly, old woman who, his wife informs him, is one of her servants.

The bride announces that there will be dancing, and retreats to her room to change into her ball gown. Emil tells Roderich that he is going to sneak into her room from a back entrance to surprise her. Roderich and his friends take this opportunity to change into grotesque Carnival costumes they brought with them to play a trick on Emil. Suddenly there is a scream, and the wedding guests witness the bride stagger from her room in a white dress, breasts bared, chased by her groom who stabs her to death. Emil tumbles over the railing with the old woman and dies. As he dies in Roderich's arms, we learn that he reacted so violently because Roderich's costume, which included a bodice like the one the old woman had worn in the cemetery, triggered the memory of the fateful night when he witnessed the sacrifice of the little girl by his wife and the old woman.

The impact of Lothar's story on the group of listeners is strong and varied, but it is strongest among the women. Clara is appalled, claiming that she cannot even think clearly, she is so horrified. Manfred disagrees, and an argument ensues about how best to critique a story of horror and fantasy. While the women react with emotion, disgust, and fear at the subject matter, Manfred seeks to justify horror, fantasy, and suspense as valid literary techniques, making it clear that the listeners knew they would be hearing a horror story. He proceeds to distinguish fantasy from real-world horror, which is much worse: "Die Phantasie, die Dichtung also wollt ihr verklagen? Aber eure Wirklichkeit! Tut doch nur die Augen auf [. . .] und seht, daß es dort, vor euren Augen, hinter eurem Rücken [. . .] weit schlimmer hergeht" (Fantasy, poetry is what you criticize? But what of your reality! Just open your eyes [. . .] and see that there, right before your eyes, behind your back [. . .] much worse things happen) (Frank 1985, 242). With Manfred's voice, Tieck addresses the issue of defining the fantasy of the Gothic sublime and an aesthetic of horror against real-world horrors, which Edmund Burke first presented in his book, *A Philosophical Enquiry into the Origin of Our Ideas of the Sublime and Beautiful* (1757), and which Kant expanded on in his *Critique of Judgment* (1790).

In his story, Tieck combines obvious elements from vampire literature, especially the appearance and demeanor of vampires (pallor, bright red lips, unnatural stiffness, licking blood from the victim's neck), with black magic. Though the connection between vampirism and witchcraft may not be immediately clear, their roots in European cultural history have been linked since ancient times. Many pagan religions had vampire figures among their demonic beings that also demonstrated similarities to the lamia of ancient Greece (Melton 1999, 685). As Christianity spread throughout Europe, pagan gods were generally disregarded as imaginary; the Church claimed that they simply did not exist. The Church had similar ideas about vampires; though they were known to the Church, they were regarded as imaginary pagan fantasies, an approach to paganism that prevailed for the first millennium AD (Melton 1999, 685). By the fifteenth century the Roman Catholic Church had established a number of inquisitions to address issues of heresy and apostasy (Burman 1985, 15–16). However, when Pope Innocent VIII issued the papal bull "Summis desiderantes affectibus" in 1484, which allowed witchcraft to be considered apostasy if it could be connected with devil worship, the demonization of the otherwise harmless pagan fantasy of witchcraft could be open to inquisition. The Dominican monks Heinrich Kramer and Jacob Sprenger used this papal bull to justify their efforts to persecute witches by including it as an introductory piece in their publication, *Malleus Maleficarum* (1487), suggesting that the Church approved of the methods they put forth in their book.

The demonization of vampirism occurred in the seventeenth century when Fr. Leo Allatius wrote his treatise, "De Graecorum hodie quirundam opinationibus" (1645), and the French Jesuit priest Fr. François Richard wrote "Relation de ce qui s'est passé a Saint-Erini Isle de l'Archipel" (1657) in response to stories of the Greek vrykolakas.[1] In their essays, Allatius and Richard sought to link vampirism to witchcraft as the work of the devil. Richard in particular made a concerted effort in his treatise to connect vampirism with characteristics and observations that Kramer and Sprenger emphasized in the *Malleus*, in an effort to link vampirism undeniably with the already demonized witchcraft. For example, in the *Malleus*, Kramer and Sprenger argue that three things must be present for witchcraft to be performed: the devil, witches, and the permission of God. Similarly, according to Richard, for vampirism to take place, the following had to be present: the devil, a corpse, and the permission of God (Melton 1999, 687). The demonization of witches and the connection that was made soon afterward to vampirism defined both as evils that opposed the Church. As such, they could be resisted and controlled with the assistance of sacred and blessed objects, such as the crucifix, the Eucharist wafer, and holy water (Melton 1999, 688). Though Tieck did not employ any outwardly obvious characteristics of the vampire in his story, such as a corpse that rises from the grave to torment or kill loved ones, he makes an important historical connection between the demonization of witchcraft and the demonization of vampirism when he brings the two together in the image of the witch/vampire bride in his story, "Love Magic." This is suggestive of some knowledge of the persecution of witches that would inform his work on his novella, *Der Hexensabbat* (The Witches' Sabbath;1832).

Moreover, Tieck uses the vampire in his story as the embodiment of such societal anxieties and fears as anonymity in the big city and the unawareness of a person's true nature. The reader knows from the beginning of the story that Emil is not a very socially inclined person, and Roderich even goes as far as to call his friend's behavior an illness. Emil is a stranger who is lonely in a city full of people, and though he has the opportunity to meet the woman he has admired from afar, this situation causes him anxieties. The solution seems to be to confide in his more outgoing friend, who is unavailable when most needed. The anonymity of the city and the protagonist's related anxieties become most evident when he attends the masquerade ball, and especially in the poem he writes of his experiences there. Of course, the symbolic value of the masquerade ball and people in masks is that no one is who they seem to be; a person's true identity has to be questioned, but this is natural and expected. The images Emil associates with the ball in the poem that he writes upon returning home are images of a dizzying chaos of people and dance that create a confusing atmosphere of uncertainty. Emil's entire awareness of the young woman who lives across the street is limited to what he believes he sees from his position in his apartment. He sees and admires the young woman every day, creating an image of her in his mind as a good person who is caring for an orphan, but he does not truly know her because he does not interact with her in any other way. When he does become aware of her true nature as a practitioner of black magic who is a willing participant in a human sacrifice, his psychological reaction is to lose consciousness; he retreats into the more comfortable state of unawareness which is symbolically represented in his amnesia.

In its nature as a monster that is easily recognizable as a human being by its outward appearance, a human-seeming monster, the vampire is a particularly useful metaphor to express anxieties associated with the "known unknown"—things or people are not always as they seem, and sometimes they are much more horrifying than they at first appear to be. This is especially true in Tieck's story.

E. T. A. HOFFMANN: "VAMPIRISMUS" (VAMPIRISM) (1821)

E. T. A. Hoffmann's story, "Vampirismus," is a tale that the character Cyprian tells in volume 4, part 8 of Hoffmann's collection of stories, *Die Serapionsbrüder* (The Serapion Brethren) which was published between 1819 and 1821. Though it is likely that Hoffmann had begun writing this story before 1821, or that he had at least completed preliminary work on the story before he finally published it in the final volume of *Die Serapionsbrüder*, this cannot be verified (Segebrecht and Segebrecht 2001, 1633). When Hoffmann's friend Adalbert Chamisso returned to Berlin in 1818 after having traveled for three years, Hoffmann decided to re-establish the literary group, known as the "Seraphinenorden," to which he and Chamisso had belonged before Chamisso left on his travels (Brown 2006, 8–9). At the same time, Hoffmann was conceiving the frame narrative for *Die Serapionsbrüder*, for which he had chosen St. Serapion as a patron saint for the fictional literary group (Brown 2006, 9). The structure of *Die Serapionsbrüder* as a collection of stories told by a group of friends who gather to tell stories, discuss literature, and critique it, is modeled after Ludwig Tieck's collection of stories, *Phantasus*. By converging the reality of his own personal experiences with the literary group, Seraphinenorden, which coincidentally became the "Serapionsorden," with the fictional frame narrative for his collection, Hoffmann was able to skillfully interweave the real world with an imaginary world, thus implementing the Serapiontic Principle of "basing a fictional narrative on [. . .] solid foundations" for the structure of his collection (Brown 2006, 9). As it is presented in the discussions by the various members of this literary group in Hoffmann's frame narrative, the Serapiontic Principle is quite complex. In their discussions of the stories that are told, the members discuss aesthetics, literary techniques, and literary themes, always reflecting on suitability based on the Serapiontic Principle (Brown 2006, 185). Far from dismissing certain popular occult topics, such as controversial theories about hypnotism, somnambulism, and even vampires, the members of this literary group see a world of possibilities for the artist in these areas of inquiry into fantasy and the psyche (Brown 2006, 160). In volume 4 of *Die Serapionsbrüder*, Hoffmann addresses his personal interest in and knowledge of the vampire superstition and the vampire reports that were published almost one hundred years earlier when the brethren discuss vampires, and one of the members, Cyprian, tells a vampire story.

A discussion of the vampire in literature begins when one of the friends or brethren, Sylvester, praises Lord Byron's work, especially his tendency toward horror, and mentions that he did not dare read Byron's story, "The Vampire," which has since been correctly attributed to Byron's physician, John Polidori, out of fear of this creature that sucks the blood of the living (Segebrecht and Segebrecht 2001, 1115). Another member of the group of friends, Lothar, laughs at this and exclaims that a poet of Sylvester's caliber should be more familiar with stories of ghosts, witches, magic, and the like, and should probably also have some experience in the practice of the magical arts in order to be able to write about it, because these are useful topics for literature. In order to prove his own knowledge in matters of supernatural horror, Lothar refers his friend to an interesting little work on vampires: Michael Ranft's popular treatise, "Traktat vom Kauen und Schmatzen der Todten in Gräbern" (Treatise on the Chewing and Smacking of the Dead in Their Graves).[2] He recommends Ranft's essay as a fine source for comprehensive information on vampirism, should Sylvester want to inform himself thoroughly. The extended title Lothar gives this work is "M. Michael Ranft's Diaconi zu Nebra, Traktat von dem Kauen und Schmatzen der Todten in Gräbern, worin die wahre Beschaffenheit derer Hungarischen Vampyrs und Blutsauger gezeigt, auch alle von dieser Materie bisher zum Vorschein gekommene Schriften rezensirt worden" (M. Michael Ranft's Deacons of Nebra, Treatise on the Chewing and Smacking of the Dead in Their Graves, wherein the true nature of the Hungarian vampires and bloodsuckers are shown and also all writings on this topic that have thus appeared are reviewed). As far as Lothar is concerned, the title itself is an indication of how thorough the actual treatise is (Segebrecht and Segebrecht 2001, 1116). He confirms Sylvester's understanding of the vampire by summarizing Ranft's essay, which identifies a vampire as a person who rises from the grave to suck the blood of the living as they sleep, who in turn become vampires, so that entire villages are transformed into vampires, according to this and other reports from Hungary. He also mentions Ranft's observation that vampires can be destroyed if they are exhumed, staked through the heart, and finally burned (Segebrecht and Segebrecht 2001, 1116). In his summary of Ranft's treatise, Hoffmann focuses on the observations that Ranft made of the vampire superstition through Lothar, but he does not address the premise of Ranft's work, which was to find a rational explanation based on scientific inquiry for this superstition. This is understandable because it is one of the purposes of the brethren to discuss the value of such a topic as vampires for literature, according to the Serapiontic Principle they lay forth in their discussions. Moreover, these reports that Lothar explains in great detail establish a solid foundation in reality for the literary vampire, which is an important feature of the Serapiontic Principle.

Lothar continues his discussion of the vampire reports by mentioning a letter that he attributes to a military officer, an ensign in Prince Alexander's regiment, written in Belgrade to a famous doctor in Leipzig who is not named here. It is possible that the letter Lothar mentions here is in fact a reference to the popular vampire story, "Visum et repertum (Arnod Paole)," by Johannes Flückinger,[3] especially because it was also written in Belgrade and signed by officers from Prince Alexander's regiment, although the story that Lothar tells is not the same one that Flückinger relates in "Visum et repertum." At the end of his report, Flückinger credits his assistants, and two officers of Prince Alexander's regiment confirm with their signatures the veracity of the document (Sturm and Völker 1968, 456). However, Lothar gives the author of the letter the name Sigismund Alexander Friedrich von Kottwitz (Segebrecht and Segebrecht 2001, 1117). Through Lothar's lengthy explanation of his knowledge of the vampire superstition through documentation of vampire investigations in central Europe, Hoffmann makes the reader aware of his own familiarity with this cultural history of the vampire, especially when he lets Lothar remark correctly: "Überhaupt beschäftigte sich damals das Militär ganz ungemein mit dem Vampyrismus" (Actually the military was quite involved with vampirism back then) (Segebrecht and Segebrecht 2001, 1117). Far from being "ungestaltetes Material" (formless material), as Wulf and Ursula Segebrecht suggest in their commentary (Segebrecht and Segebrecht 2001, 1638), Lothar's exposé on Ranft's treatise connects the vampire theme in literature to its origins in the real world of the eighteenth-century vampire debates.

In reaction to Sylvester's remark that the mere idea of vampirism is exceedingly repulsive, Cyprian believes that an imaginative poet with "poetic tact" can take this idea of vampirism and create something that "die tiefen Schauer jenes geheimnisvollen Grauens erregt, das in unserer eigenen Brust wohnt, und berührt von den elektrischen Schlägen einer dunkeln Geisterwelt den Sinn erschüttert, ohne ihn zu verstören" (excites the deep chills of that mysterious horror that lives in our own breast and, touched by the electrical shocks of a dark spirit world, rattles the senses without unsettling them) (Segebrecht and Segebrecht 2001, 1117). Theodor reminds Cyprian that he need not offer an "apology for horror" because so many of the greatest poets, especially Shakespeare, had already mastered the art of affecting a reader's disposition without causing actual distress. In addition to Shakespeare, he names Ludwig Tieck's work and his story, "Liebeszauber" (Love Magic), in particular, and Heinrich von Kleist's story, "Das Bettelweib von Locarno" (The Beggarwoman from Locarno; 1810), as further examples of mastery in creating this atmosphere of the Gothic sublime in their work (Segebrecht and Segebrecht 2001, 1118). This discussion of vampirism reminds Cyprian of a story that he either heard or read, which he proceeds to tell to the group of friends.

The story Cyprian tells is about the young Count Hyppolit, whose father had just passed away, so the Count has returned from collecting his substantial inheritance and is busy renovating his residence and the grounds. His uncle reminds him that he should probably start seeking a wife, and soon afterward a distant relative of his father's, known only as the Baroness, pays him a visit, accompanied by her daughter, Aurelie. When the Count hears the Baroness's name announced, he recalls how much his father despised this woman. In fact his father's feelings about her were best described as indignation, revulsion, and loathing, though no one could explain it. His father never gave a detailed explanation about his dislike of this woman, insisting that there are certain things that are best left unspoken. When Hyppolit meets the Baroness, he senses the dread and horror that his father described, though it has nothing to do with her physical appearance. As she speaks with him, he is very aware of how repugnant she seems to him, even though her general appearance is appealing. However, as a good host he welcomes her to stay at his residence, especially after she tells him of her dire financial situation. In particular, Hyppolit is interested in her very attractive daughter. When he takes the Baroness's hands in his own to welcome her officially to his home, he is shocked at how cold her hands are and at that moment her hands grow stiff in his hands (Segebrecht and Segebrecht 2001, 1122). Aurelie apologizes and explains that her mother suffers from cataleptic attacks, and that this will pass in a few moments, which it does.

Despite this uncanny initial encounter, the Baroness's strange demeanor, and her unusual practice of taking nighttime walks through the park toward the cemetery, Hyppolit falls in love with Aurelie and asks for her hand in marriage. On the morning of their wedding day, however, the Baroness is found unconscious and face down in the cemetery, and finally dies after attempts to resuscitate her fail. The wedding is postponed for several weeks, and Aurelie continues to be visibly distressed, not so much by her mother's death but rather by an unknown anxiety or fear that is cause for concern for the Count. Finally, Aurelie decides that she must tell her husband about her background, so that he might understand her anxieties. Aurelie's story within the story "Vampirismus" covers the middle portion of Hoffmann's carefully constructed narrative. In her telling of the story of her childhood, Aurelie reveals the horrors of the life of neglect and actual imprisonment she endured at the hands of her mother after her father died.

When Aurelie was sixteen years old, her mother met a man who visited frequently and finally took up residence in their home. Aurelie found it strange that the man appeared so youthful, despite the fact that he was apparently forty years old. Upon his arrival in their home, the Baroness's financial situation improves significantly, but she continues to neglect her daughter. Much to Aurelie's dismay, the man takes a sexual interest in her, and her mother makes it clear that she expects her daughter to give in to his will, since he makes it possible for them to live in luxury. One night Aurelie is witness to an assault on her mother by this man, whom the police arrest. After a while it becomes necessary for the Baroness and Aurelie to leave their residence, which is why the Baroness sought out her distant relative, Count Hyppolit. Aurelie ends her story by telling the Count that her mother was surprisingly angry when she informed her mother of her happiness in her developing relationship with the Count. In fact, the Baroness cursed her daughter, and this is the source of Aurelie's anxieties; Aurelie is too distraught, however, and is unable to finish repeating the curse that her mother cast on her (Segebrecht and Segebrecht 2001, 1129–30).

Shortly after she confesses her tragic story, Hyppolit notices disturbing changes in his wife's appearance and her demeanor; the spark in her eyes disappears, she develops a deathly pallor and, more striking than this, she develops a feeling of disgust for food, especially meat. The doctor believes that these are signs that she may be pregnant, and proceeds to tell a gruesome story about a woman who killed her husband and ate his flesh, which sparks Aurelie's interest. Aurelie's condition worsens, and Hyppolit becomes especially alarmed when a servant informs him that his wife has been observed leaving the castle late at night and not returning until the morning. It occurs to Hyppolit that of late he had been falling into a particularly deep sleep at midnight, and he wonders if his wife has been drugging him. He fears that the final words of her mother has had an effect on Aurelie, or that she might be having an affair. In order to see for himself where his wife goes when she leaves the castle at night, he does not drink the tea she gives him before going to bed, and feigns sleep.[4] When she leaves the castle that night he follows her to the cemetery. To his profound horror, the Count observes a group of half-naked women devouring a corpse, and his wife is among them. In deathly fear and horror at what he observed, the Count rides home and finds his wife asleep, as if nothing had happened. He tries to rationalize what he saw by convincing himself that it was a nightmare, and that the hem of her dress is wet because she might have been sleepwalking. However, when

Aurelie is once again repulsed by the meat that is served for dinner, Count Hyppolit recalls all the horrors of the previous night and calls her a cursed product of hell (Segebrecht and Segebrecht 2001, 1133). Aurelie reacts by attacking him and biting him in the breast. Hyppolit kills her and goes mad.

After a stunned silence, Lothar and Theodor comment on Cyprian's telling of this story. Lothar is impressed with the sheer horror of the story. Theodor, however, is careful to point out that Cyprian's artistic skills in telling his horror story were evident in his ability to build suspense and create an atmosphere of horror by suggesting scenes of horror rather than going into too much graphic detail that would otherwise make the story repugnant to the cultured reader. Theodor concludes his critique by suggesting that, in contrast to the version of this story that he had read, which went into graphic detail that disgusted him, Cyprian never lost sight of Serapion's principles in the telling of his story (Segebrecht and Segebrecht 2001, 1134). Lothar had already established the solid foundation of the vampire theme in his discussion of the vampire reports before Cyprian told his story. This foundation in reality, combined with the skillfully constructed and suspenseful narration that is lauded by Lothar for its tasteful approach, seems to be Hoffmann's way of presenting a model for an aesthetic of horror in literature.

In "Vampirismus," Hoffmann introduces the aristocratic vampire into German literature in the Baroness's implied nature as a vampire and her daughter's confirmed nature as a vampire. These vampire aristocrats are also associated with a whole array of social taboos, making a larger association with the moral corruption of the upper classes unavoidable. The female vampires in this story are either the aggressors or the victims, whether implied, suspected, or witnessed, in such wide-ranging social taboos as cannibalism, necrophilia, bigamy, incest, infidelity, physical and mental abuse, parental neglect, and sexual assault. As such, Hoffmann's vampires are truly the cultural bodies that reflect social anxieties, fears, and taboos that Jeffrey Jerome Cohen and Noël Carroll put forth in their theories about the monster and horror literature (Carroll 1990, 207; Cohen 1996, 4). Their bodies are essentially horrific landscapes that are composed of some of the most appalling human actions of depravity, but presented in a very human-seeming, even physically appealing, package. The author is the artist who puts together this composite image, so that the reader is faced with an actual embodiment of social fears, anxieties, and taboos. The sense of repulsion the Count and others feel in the presence of the Baroness in particular has less to do with her physical appearance than it does with an instinctive repulsion toward a person who seems to be unnatural.

Hoffmann's skill in building an aura of mystery and suspense about the mysterious nature of the Baroness is initially evident in the Count's memory of his father's vague warning about this distant relative, his remark that it might be better to keep silent about it than to speak of it (Segebrecht and

Segebrecht 2001, 1120). Aurelie's first memory of her mother is that the Baroness took her away from the home she knew after her father died, only to keep her daughter locked in her room when she entertained the man she calls "der Fremde" ("the stranger"). Aurelie's memories are a collection of sporadic observations and often terrifying experiences at the hands of her mother and the stranger. The dual taboos of bigamy and incest are introduced in the story when the stranger, who has been living in the Baroness's house in an implied marriage, shows a sexual interest in Aurelie. This is intensified in his attempted sexual assault of Aurelie, which she is fortunately able to avoid by pushing him away and escaping to her room. The abuse turns to mental abuse when her mother chastises her daughter for resisting the advances of the man who supports them financially (Segebrecht and Segebrecht 2001, 1126–27). The stranger's unusually youthful appearance for a man who is probably forty years old suggests his nature as a vampire, which is a further indication of the Baroness's necrophilia in her relationship with him. Throughout the story, the Baroness's aura of repulsiveness has a profound effect on people, such as her own daughter, Hyppolit, and Hyppolit's father before him, though no one can explain it. When Aurelie begins to exhibit similarities in appearance and demeanor with her mother, and especially when she is observed leaving the castle at night like her mother did, Hyppolit is torn between memories of the dreadful Baroness and suspicions of infidelity. All of the observations, however, are based on the individual characters' perceptions of what is happening. The narrator never steps in to explain what the reader (and Cyprian's listeners) should understand, and this is how Hoffmann creates suspense through Cyprian's telling of the story. The horror reaches a climax when Hyppolit observes his wife in the cannibalistic act of devouring a corpse in the cemetery, which at the same time suggests the solution to the mystery of the Baroness's strange midnight wanderings when she was alive.

In his masterful composition of this vampire story, Hoffmann combines the reality of the reports of vampirism in central Europe from the 1730s, images of necrophilia and cannibalism from German vampire folklore, and contemporary social taboos to create a modern monster. His monster is truly a modern composite of opposites: old and new, victim and aggressor, disclosure and secrecy, good will and evil intent, and it reminds us of Mary Shelley's *Frankenstein: or, the Modern Prometheus*, written only a few years earlier in 1818. Like Shelley's monster, Hoffmann's vampire holds up a mirror to society and tells the reader about the social ills that created such a monster.

ERNST BENJAMIN SALOMO RAUPACH: "LAßT DIE TODTEN RUHEN" (WAKE NOT THE DEAD, OR THE BRIDE OF THE GRAVE; 1823)

The authorship of the story, "Laßt die Todten ruhen"[5] (Wake Not the Dead) has been falsely attributed to Ludwig Tieck since 1973 when Peter Haining included this story in volume 2 of his popular and widely referenced collection of horror stories, *Gothic Tales of Terror*.[6] In fact, Tieck's contemporary, the German author and playwright Ernst Benjamin Salomo Raupach, wrote this story in 1823. German scholars since the late nineteenth century have attributed this story to Raupach with no mention of Tieck in connection with the original German story or the English translation, yet British and American scholars or collectors of Gothic horror literature and the vampire in literature have consistently attributed this story to Tieck, one of Germany's most highly regarded Romantic authors. Considering the popularity of the English translation of this story, which is evident from the story's presence in influential British and American anthologies of European Gothic horror literature (Haining 1972, 93–121) and widely referenced critical editions, encyclopedias, and other scholarly works on Gothic horror literature and the vampire (Aguirre 1990, 135–36; Bartlett and Idriceanu 2008, 28; Bloom 1998, 160; Bunson 1993, 277; Frost 1998, 37–38; Melton 1999, 255; Potter 2005, 189), it is necessary here to establish once and for all the correct authorship of the story, leaving no doubt that the rightful author is Ernst Benjamin Salomo Raupach and not Ludwig Tieck.

The story "Wake Not the Dead" was first published in the collection of stories, *Minerva: Taschenbuch für das Jahr 1823* as "Ein Märchen von D. Ernst Raupach" (A Fairy Tale by D. Ernst Raupach). In his seminal work, *Grundrisz zur Geschichte der deutschen Dichtung* (Outline of the History of German Literature), Karl Goedeke presents a detailed account of Raupach's life and work, in which he also critiques Raupach's "Wake Not the Dead" (Goedeke 1989, 650, 661). The German literary scholar, Stefan Hock, also references *Minerva* as the original source of Raupach's story before he summarizes the plot of the story and critiques it in his book *Die Vampyrsagen und ihre Verwertung in der deutschen Literatur* (The Vampire Legends and their Application in German Literature) from 1900 (Hock 1977, 108). In the second edition of Goedeke's *Grundrisz*, published in 1905 as a posthumous expansion of the work that Goedeke started with his multivolume *Grundrisz*, the editor, Edmund Goetze, in turn references Stefan Hock as an additional source for information on Raupach's story (Goedeke 1989, 661). Interestingly, despite Goedeke's, Hock's, and Goetze's unquestioning acknowledgments of Raupach as the author based on the story's original publication in *Minerva: Taschenbuch für das Jahr 1823*, subsequent scholars and editors of anthologies from Great Britain and the United States have erroneously acknowledged Ludwig Tieck as the author of the story, with no reference to Raupach. In fact, Matthew Bunson claims that the story was "written by Johann Ludwig Tieck in Germany in 1800, but not published in English until 1823, when it was included in the three-volume anthology, *Popular Tales and Romances of the Northern Nations*" (Bunson 1993, 277). It is true that the English translation of the story, "Wake Not the Dead," was first published in the anthology Bunson references, but in this particular anthology from 1823 no author is attributed with the individual stories other than through vague acknowledgment in the preface as an author in the collection. In fact, the only mention of Tieck as an author in this collection appears in the preface in one sentence: "Lebrecht and Tieck are the authors of many beautiful legends, but they have generally trusted to their own fancy instead of building themselves on ancient traditions" (Simpkin W. and R. Marshall 1823, xii). There is no other mention of Tieck or his individual works in this multivolume anthology, nor is his name ascribed to any story as the author.

It is likely that the confusion about the authorship of this particular story arose for the simple reason that the story "Wake Not the Dead" directly precedes the English translation of Tieck's famous story, "Der blonde Eckbert" ("Fair Eckbert" in the anthology) in volume 1 of *Popular Tales and Romances*, and Tieck is named in the preface among other famous German authors whose translated works appear in the anthology, though Raupach is not named. Other than this misguided assumption, it is not clear how Tieck could have been identified as the author of "Wake Not the Dead" in this widely referenced anthology, which is the original publication of the English translation. Interestingly, 150 years after the publication of *Popular Tales and Romances*, Peter Haining included the English translation of Raupach's story in his anthology of horror stories, but with the alternate title, "The Bride of the Grave," instead of "Wake Not the Dead" (Haining 1972, 93). In fact, the English title "The Bride of the Grave" first appears in conjunction with "Wake Not the Dead" as an alternate title for Raupach's story in the anthology, *Legends of Terror!* in 1826, which suggests that Haining may have consulted this particular anthology for his collection of stories. In *Legends of Terror!* as in the earlier 1823 anthology, *Popular Tales and Romances*, neither Tieck nor Raupach is attributed with authorship. In *Legends of Terror!* some authors are identified with their works if the author was known to the editors, but this particular story is published anonymously. This is not surprising because the editors of *Legends of Terror!* do recognize *Popular Tales and Romances* as the anthology that first published "Wake Not the Dead" in English translation, and they acknowledge that they borrowed it for their anthology in an introductory paragraph to the story:

> The interest of the following tale is of a description most dark and fearful, and but few translations can convey to the English reader the romantic wildness

and spirit of the German original. We have seen several translations, but we think none of them are equal to the one given in the collection of "Popular Tales and Romances of Northern Nations," lately published by the German bookseller, Bohte, of Tavistock Street, which we take the liberty of extracting. (Sherwood, Gilbert, and Piper 1826, 129)

The indication in this introductory statement that there were several translations of Raupach's story attests to the popularity of this vampire tale in England. Moreover, the fact that the editors apparently chose this translation among many, and yet the story was published as an anonymous work, suggests that no author was ever attributed to this particular story until Haining chose to identify Tieck as the author.

In an introductory paragraph that precedes the translated story in his 1973 anthology, Haining writes that he selected "The Bride of the Grave" "from the body of Tieck's work," though he does not mention any specific sources from Tieck's "body of work" that he apparently consulted. Despite this unsubstantiated reference to Tieck's authorship, scholars since 1973 have been willing to accept Haining's claim that Tieck wrote this story. Anthologies, encyclopedias, critical editions, and other scholarly publications on Gothic literature by British and American authors that do ascribe the story's authorship to Tieck ultimately cite Haining as the initial source for this story, or cite others whose work references Haining. In his article, "The Intellectual Functions of Gothic Fiction: Poe's 'Ligeia' and Tieck's 'Wake Not the Dead,'" Paul Lewis goes a bit further in identifying the initial source for the translation when he states in his notes: "A widely available source for this tale is *Gothic Tales of Terror* [. . .] by Peter Haining. [. . .] 'Wake Not the Dead' was translated into English at least a decade before Poe wrote 'Ligeia.' This translation appears in *Popular Tales of the Northern Nations* [. . .] and is the basis of the text Haining uses in the edition I cite above" (Lewis 1979, 219). As mentioned above, it is more likely that Haining's source for the story was indeed *Legends of Terror!* since he uses the alternate title, "The Bride of the Grave," from the latter anthology for his own collection. This is, however, speculative, as is Lewis's claim that *Popular Tales and Romances* was Haining's source, because Haining does not cite a source other than to say that he "selected it from Tieck's body of work" in his introductory paragraph to the story. Moreover, although Lewis draws the following conclusion: "About Poe's having read the story by Tieck in question here I have been able to read nothing, but this is not conclusive because Poe, always busy accusing others of plagiarism, was careful to conceal his own borrowings" (Lewis 1979, 219), it is more likely that Poe borrowed from, or was influenced by, the anonymously published story from one of the previously mentioned anthologies from 1823 or 1826. This may explain why Poe never mentions Tieck nor anyone else as an inspiration for "Ligeia."

German scholars do not mention the story "Laßt die Todten ruhen" or the English translation "Wake Not the Dead" / "The Bride of the Grave" in connection with Tieck's work, and there is also no mention of the story or its translation in Tieck's letters. Based on the available facts, it is my conclusion that the story "Wake Not the Dead" / "The Bride of the Grave," which has been widely referenced in anthologies, reference works, critical editions, and other scholarly work on the vampire in literature and Gothic horror literature as a story by Ludwig Tieck, is in fact the English translation of Raupach's story from 1823. Attributing authorship to Tieck by British and American scholars and anthologists since at least 1973 has been misguided and perpetuated until now.

Ernst Benjamin Salomo Raupach was born on May 21, 1784, in Straupitz, a village near Liegnitz in Silesia. He attended the University of Halle from 1801 until 1804 with the intention of studying theology, but during the course of his studies he pursued his interests in history, Latin, and mathematics, and taught himself French. His primary interests in philosophy were limited to the field of metaphysics, though he also attended lectures in aesthetics, logic, and ethics early in his academic career. He was particularly well read in the works of Voltaire and Rousseau, and translated many works by Lafontaine into French. After several years' employment as a private tutor, first for a family in Groß-Wiersewitz near Liegnitz (1804) and then in St. Petersburg for a family where his older brother, Friedrich, was also a tutor (1804–1814), Raupach earned his PhD from the University of Halle on November 28, 1814 (Goedeke 1989, 646–47, 658). He began his writing career in 1810 and is best known as a very prolific dramatist. After the education of his private student was completed, Raupach remained in St. Petersburg as a private teacher for foreign languages, history, geography, and literature. In 1816 he accepted a position at the Institute for Pedagogy in St. Petersburg, and married Cäcilie von Wildermeth. She and their newborn son died one year later. Raupach returned to Germany in 1823 and almost immediately accepted an invitation by Luise Duchess of Saxe-Weimar-Eisenach to read a selection of his dramatic work at court. He was hopeful that he would be able to begin a fruitful interaction with Goethe while he was in Weimar, but instead Goethe's reception of him was polite and distant. Understandably, this angered Raupach, and he altered his plans to settle in Weimar, opting instead to live in Berlin (Goedeke 1989, 649).

Raupach was indeed a prolific playwright, having produced for the Berlin Court Theater a total of ninety-eight plays between 1820 and 1842, most of which were historical dramas and twenty-one of which were never published (Goedeke 1989, 657–58). This is not surprising when we consider that his primary goal in writing for the theater was to rid the German theater of foreign influences, especially from France, and bring German plays back to the German theater. He was less concerned with attaining a high level of aesthetic value in his work than he was with drawing people to the theater with entertaining productions, and in this he was quite successful (Goedeke 1989, 652). Though Raupach's dramatic work is not generally critically acclaimed (Goedeke 1989, 650–57; Hock 1977, 110–12), Goedeke does recognize his talent for writing dramatic roles with the actors' abilities in mind, and reserves more favorable criticism for Raupach's comedies than he does for his historical dramas. His scathing review of Raupach's prose work says as much about his talents as an author as it does about the contemporary disdain by many German critics for much of the Gothic horror literature that was published in Germany in the nineteenth century.[7]

In his story, Raupach continues the tradition of the female vampire that Goethe introduced with his ballad, "The Bride of Corinth," in 1797. However, in his story, Raupach combines the motifs of the dead lover returning with motifs of sorcery, necromancy, and the danger of unbridled longing and lust for the deceased. In this story, the nobleman Walter loses his first wife, Brunhilde, whom he loved very much. He remarries a very good woman, Swanhilde, and has children with her, but as the years pass, he thinks back on his wedded bliss with Brunhilde and longs again for that passion and intimacy, both physical and spiritual, which he does not find with Swanhilde. As he laments Brunhilde's death over her grave, he encounters a sorcerer who assures him that he can raise the dead, but that this is not advisable after a lengthy discussion about the morality of Walter's request. He warns him with the words, "Wake not the dead!" and leaves after telling Walter to return the following night.

After spending the entire following day in desperate anticipation, Walter repeats his request to the sorcerer to reanimate Brunhilde, and the sorcerer repeats his warning, "Wake not the dead!" Walter must wait another day, and on the third night the sorcerer repeats his warning again and finally raises Brunhilde from the dead, assisted by the elements that convene in a big storm around the gravesite. After she rises from the dead, Walter takes her to one of his more isolated castles where they stay for two weeks while she slowly adjusts to the light, becoming more beautiful and youthful and less like a corpse as time passes. When her former beauty is fully restored, Walter is once again attracted to her and makes sexual advances toward her. She thwarts his advances, demanding that he wait another seven days until the next full moon. When this time comes he makes advances again, and she reciprocates to a point, but then informs him that his (and her) desire will not be fulfilled until she is restored to the throne as his wife. Walter divorces Swanhilde and sends her home to her father without the children, in accordance with the local law. For some time, Brunhilde and Walter live together in passionate bliss, though Walter is oblivious to the fact that his lover has been draining the blood from all the children and youths in the surrounding villages, until she has no choice but to focus her attention on Walter's children and finally Walter in order to survive as a vampire. When Brunhilde begins to feed on Walter's blood, his energy and thus his passion for her deteriorates and he spends less time with her and increasingly more time in nature.

One day when he is resting under a tree, a bird drops a root at his feet. He picks it up and takes a bite, throwing it away because of the bitter taste. The effect of this magical root is that Walter is not affected by Brunhilde's hypnotic seduction of him and awakens at night to find her sucking blood from his breast. He recoils in repulsion and flees the castle, seeking refuge in his other castle. Unfortunately for Walter, Brunhilde's spell over him allows her to find him, so that he awakens in her arms in the morning. He seeks refuge in a cave, but this is also unsuccessful and he awakens in her arms again. On this third night he notices the full moon and remembers that the sorcerer had mentioned that Walter could meet him at a crossroads, if he ever felt repulsed by the revenant he has awakened from the dead. The sorcerer informs Walter that he must kill Brunhilde with a dagger in the night of the new moon in two weeks. Until this time, Walter must remain in the cave, which the sorcerer protects with a magical circle. When the time comes, Walter kills Brunhilde and speaks the curse that he must also repeat after she has died, if he should ever think of her again (Raupach 1823, 81). Once he kills his vampire lover, he agonizes over the loss of Swanhilde and his children. He seeks forgiveness from Swanhilde, but she is unable to reunite with him when she discovers that he allowed her children to die.

Shortly thereafter he encounters a huntress dressed in black who bears a remarkable resemblance to Swanhilde, though she is a brunette like Brunhilde. He is intrigued by this mysterious composite of the two very different women whom he once loved, and invites her to his castle together with her entourage. After one month of restored frivolity, Walter asks her to marry him and she does. The story ends abruptly when she turns into a snake in his arms on their wedding night and crushes him to death. The snake (or dragon) sprays fire and escapes as the castle is engulfed in flames, and a voice calls to Walter as he dies: "Wake not the dead!" (Raupach 1823, 88).

All potential suspense that is one of the most common features of the vampire poetry and prose discussed thus far, and of Gothic horror literature in general, especially with regard to the gradual revelation of the vampire figure's true identity, is lost with Raupach's story. From the very beginning of the narrative, the reader knows that Walter plans to reanimate his deceased lover in order to rekindle the physical intimacy and passion he remembers from his marriage to Brunhilde and which he misses with his current wife. There is no sense of uncertainty about the nature of this woman as a vampire, as there was in the more skillfully constructed suspenseful narratives in the poetry and in the prose works by Tieck and Hoffmann. In fact, Raupach does not leave anything to the reader's imagination when he allows the narrator to reveal every detail about Brunhilde's vampire nature, her need for blood from youths in order to restore her energy and youthful appearance, her method of taking sustenance from her victims before she actually attacks, and even her cursed existence.

A moralizing tone is present throughout the story, especially in the words of the sorcerer early in the narrative when he initially berates Walter for his expressed desire to raise Brunhilde from the dead, only to let Walter know that he can indeed perform this act.

When the sorcerer does finally raise Brunhilde from the dead, he addresses her directly, making her nature as a vampire undeniable to the reader and to Walter: "Trinke, Schläferin, trinke warmes Blut, daß das Herz wieder schlage in deiner Brust" (Drink, sleeper, drink warm blood, so that your heart will once again beat in your breast) (Raupach 1823, 48). Raupach's moralizing narrator does not even leave any doubt about the magical properties of a root that a bird (the sorcerer in disguise) drops at his feet to protect him from this vampire's attack. The author's purpose seems to be to instill a sense of repulsion in the reader in a consistently deliberate and moralizing manner, rather than to build suspense about the vampire figure specifically, and in this he is successful. This moralizing tone seems to coincide with the apparent didactic goals of the *Minerva: Taschenbuch* as a publication directed toward women, which is evident when Wilhelm Blumenhagen addresses the series' female readers directly in his introduction to this edition (Raupach 1823, vi).

The overriding themes that Raupach connects with his vampire figure and Walter's desire for her are the social taboos of necrophilia, adultery, and bigamy (Hock 1977, 110) that are evident in Walter's actions from the very beginning: "Oft nun am Abend, statt das Lager seiner Gattin zu suchen, ging er hinaus zu Brunhildens Gruft, ließ dort seine Klage erschallen, und fragte hinab in die taube Erde: willst du ewig schlafen?" (Often of an evening, instead of seeking the bed of his wife, he went to Brunhilde's grave and lamented, calling into the deaf earth: will you sleep forever?) (Raupach 1823, 43), When he exclaims to the sorcerer, "Sie soll nicht ruhen in kalter Erde! Sie soll ruhen an meiner heiß verlangenden Brust" (She shall not rest in the cold earth! She shall rest on my hot and lustful bosom) (Raupach 1823, 47), his necrophilic desires are even more blatant. In this regard, Raupach's story does not diverge much from contemporary literary tradition, especially in connection with vampire prose and German vampire folklore. As we have seen, Hoffmann's vampire story, though directly connected to central European vampire superstition in the discussion that precedes the telling of the story, has necrophilia as a predominant theme in connection with the vampire, Aurelie, which also connects the vampire to German folklore.[8] Besides Walter's active necrophilic desire to exhume the body of his dead lover so that she may live with him again, Raupach uses the motif of the horse in his story in a manner that is reminiscent of the Lenore legend that is fundamental to German vampire folklore and to Bürger's poem, "Lenore."[9] Like Bürger, Raupach uses the motif of the ride on horseback three times in the story: 1) when he takes Brunhilde away after she is raised from the dead (Raupach 1823, 50); 2) when Brunhilde demands that he leave his wife, Swanhilde (54); and 3) when he leaves with the sorcerer to kill Brunhilde (80). Each of the riding scenes occurs in direct or indirect connection with the vampire, with increasing intensity or speed and using similar language in a refrain-like manner at significant points in the narrative. Each of the rides on horseback also ends at one of Walter's castles. In its wording, Raupach's second rider scene is especially reminiscent of Bürger's "Lenore."[10] Raupach's application of the three rider scenes at important points in the narrative leaves little doubt about his inspiration by Bürger's poem, and thus the Lenore legend from German vampire folklore.

In the table of contents and on the story's title page in the *Minerva: Taschenbuch*, Raupach's story is identified as a "Märchen von D. Ernst Raupach" (Fairy Tale by D. Ernst Raupach), and Raupach does apply a variety of common fairy-tale motifs, such as magic in the form of the sorcerer, the magical root, the cave as a safe hiding place, a crossroads, animal helpers in the form of an eagle and a raven, and the almost excessive use of the numbers seven and three. However, as Hock correctly observes, these motifs do not always seem to meet their potential to figure prominently in the plot of the story as a more carefully constructed fairy-tale narrative would. The cave and the healing root are introduced in the story but they are quickly forgotten, and the implied supernatural aura of the "schwarze Jägerin" (dark huntress) at the end of the story is not well developed (Hock 1977, 111). Instead, these fairy-tale elements function more as superficial devices that only identify the story as a fairy tale on the surface, but fail to make a significant impact on the development of the plot. One possible exception is the threefold repetition of the rider scenes, which do move the plot along effectively.

Despite some of the negative aspects of the story that particularly concerned Hock and Goedeke, especially the lack of suspense, the excessively graphic images of the vampire's attacks, and the lack of character and plot development, Raupach's story is significant because it introduces important and very modern elements to the image of the vampire figure in the early nineteenth century. Brunhilde focuses her attacks on children and adolescents in an effort to restore her own youth, and if Walter dies before she is killed, she will continue to kill men. This image is reminiscent of the lamia from Greek mythology whose curse was to kill children, and Goethe's "Bride of Corinth" when the vampire bride explains to her mother that she must rise again to kill young people (stanza 26). Moreover, the image of Brunhilde as a vampire seductress who feeds off of children or young people predates Sheridan Le Fanu's *Carmilla* (1872) and Bram Stoker's Lucy in *Dracula*.

Brunhilde's method of attack is new to the image of the literary vampire. She anesthetizes her victims with her breath of violets, putting them into a deep sleep, and then she feeds on them. Though she sucks the blood from their breasts, as is common among the vampires from folklore, she does not kill them immediately. Her victims fade away over time, gradually losing their energy and youthful appearance until they finally waste away. This is a common trait among vampires in British literature later in the nineteenth century, especially in Stoker's *Dracula*, and has been connected with the literary representation of consumptive diseases, such as consumption, cancer, and pulmonary tuberculosis. From the standpoint of building a suspenseful narrative around the vampire figure, such a gradual wasting away of the victim produces a dramatic effect, especially at a time in the late nineteenth century when disease featured quite prominently in literature. Stoker was particularly successful in creating a suspenseful narrative around the vampire attack as a metaphor for disease, because he focused his attention in the narrative on the progression and the symptoms of the "disease." Raupach, on the other hand, only mentions that Brunhilde's victims die in this manner, but the suspense is lost in his failure to build the progression of the disease into the narrative.

Furthermore, Raupach's vampire has very modern metaphorical value as a cultural body that embodies social anxieties and fears (Cohen 1996, 4). Brunhilde is beautiful and desirable as a woman, but she is also the corruptive force that destroys the peaceful family unit that Walter has with Swanhilde and his children. In this story, the vampire's body functions symbolically as a repository for common fears about the destruction of the family due to adultery, or even bigamy, and which results in divorce and a metaphorical death of the family, especially evident in the children's deaths in the story. Walter's desire for Brunhilde is also centered completely on the passion and excitement he remembers from the early days of their marriage. Though he remembers the controlling and manipulative aspects of her personality that developed later in their marriage, his decision to ignore this in favor of once again experiencing physical love with the reanimated corpse of his wife is irrational. In this story, the social ill represented by the vampire is that unbridled passion is dangerous and unnatural, and can destroy otherwise strong social units such as the family.

Despite the negative critiques of Raupach's story by Goedeke and Hock, "Laßt die Todten ruhen" has been popular and critically acclaimed in its English translation, "Wake Not the Dead" since it first appeared in 1823 in *Popular Tales and Romances*. One of the most positive reviews of this story can be found in Manuel Aguirre's book, *The Closed Space: Horror Literature and Western Symbolism*, where the author observes that "the first definitive condensation—and still one of the best—of the myth [of vampirism] in western fiction appears to be Tieck's 'Bride of the Grave'" (Aguirre 1990,

135). Aguirre also identifies this story as "the first vampire in western prose fiction" (137). However, as we know, Tieck's vampire story "Liebeszauber" (Love Magic) is in fact the first prose work with a vampire theme.

THEODOR HILDEBRANDT: *DER VAMPYR ODER DIE TODTENBRAUT* (THE VAMPIRE OR THE BRIDE OF DEATH)

From a contemporary legal standpoint, infanticide in the eighteenth century was a crime that was committed only by women. Most eighteenth-century legal codes in the German territories were based on the *Constitutio Criminalis Carolina* of 1532, the penal code of Emperor Charles V. Infanticide was understood to be "the killing of an infant by its unwed mother in childbirth or immediately afterwards" (Fronius 2008, 94). This crime was punishable by death, which by the 1770s was beheading. The acts of concealing a pregnancy and giving birth in secret were also punishable offenses. Infanticide was the most frequent type of homicide in eighteenth-century Germany, but was nonetheless quite rare compared with other types of crimes (there were approximately fifty recorded cases per year in Prussia between 1774 and 1781 from a population of approximately 5 million) (Fronius 2008, 94).

Between 1772 and 1791 about twenty literary works featuring the infanticide motif were written in Germany; Anton Mathias Sprickmann's poem, "Ida" (1777), and August Gottlieb Meißner's poem, "Die Mörderin" (The Murderess; 1779) are especially important in the context of the child murderess as a monster. Both poems feature middle-class women who were seduced and then betrayed by their aristocratic lovers—an all-too-common theme; they give birth in secluded areas and kill the infants violently in fits of rage that suggest temporary insanity. The killing of the child in these and other poems is especially gruesome and designed to shock; for example, Ida licks the blood off her dead baby's face, an act that by this time in German literary history already evoked images of vampirism. However, there is never any doubt about Ida's underlying virtuous femininity. Her innocence and her compliant desire to please her lover, her submissiveness, feminine weakness, and obedient nature are what cause her to have sexual intercourse with her lover, not active lust or sexual desire (Fronius 2008, 95). The juxtaposition of her ideal demure disposition and her ability to commit a brutal murder combine to create an image of her as truly monstrous, because she defies conventional categorization. In the end, she represents a double female archetype of sacrifice and self-sacrifice, as do other unwed mothers in poems that were written at this time, for example, Gottfried August Bürger's ballad, "Des Pfarrers Tochter von Taubenhain" (The Daughter of the Preacher from Taubenhain; 1781). When Goethe combined this popular motif of the murderess with the new literary monster, the vampire, in his ballad, "Bride of Corinth," in 1797, he elevated the already horrifying image of the murderess to the realm of the supernatural by making her a vampire who preyed on the young. In *Faust I*, however, his child murderess, Gretchen, is presented as a pitiable, though naive young woman who stood for so many at this time as a victim of social injustice. The images of these literary child murderesses as monsters represented a very real problem in society, serving essentially as a cultural monstrous body for contemporary society's fears and anxieties.

In his novel from 1828, *Der Vampyr oder die Todtenbraut* (The Vampire or the Bride of Death), Theodor Hildebrandt assigns his female vampire and child murderess many of the same features Raupach had five years earlier (she kills children by infecting them with a consumptive affliction), but Hildebrandt's Russian vampire bride, Lodoiska, is much more than just a reanimated corpse. She is the victim of a tragic love story, and as a vampire she is compelled to rise from the grave to take revenge on Alfred, the man who betrayed her and caused her to commit suicide which, in central European and Slavic folklore, can cause a person to become a vampire. Hildebrandt seems to have based his story on a Byelorussian folktale, "How a Vampire (upir) Carried a Girl off to the Grave." In the folktale, a young woman and a young man who were in love vowed to each other that they would marry. After a year, the girl marries a wealthier and more handsome young man. The first young man—the scorned lover—returns for her and carries her off on horseback to a graveyard where he unscrews her head and takes it into the grave with him (Perkowski 1976, 115). In Hildebrandt's story there is a role reversal. Alfred promises to marry Lodoiska and even signs a contract in blood, in accordance with local custom. When he breaks this pact, Lodoiska commits suicide and is compelled to return to kill him and his loved ones. Her motivations for killing Alfred's children and his wife are personal, but as a vampire she also has no choice in the matter. Much like John Polidori's vampire character, Lord Ruthven, in his 1819 novella, *The Vampire*, Lodoiska is presented to the reader as a very complex personality, in whom melancholy, cruelty, manipulation, and a lust for power form a potent and dangerous mixture (Barkhoff 2008, 129). In response to contemporary interest in the subconscious, Hildebrandt's story is especially innovative in that it pays close attention to the female (vampire) protagonist's inner world and feelings, particularly the fact that she is a victim of betrayal.

A common thread in these stories is the "unnatural woman" (vampire), a destructive force that is able to threaten a family unit that has itself become "unnatural" because it is a broken (weakened) home, and thus susceptible to destruction. In Raupach's story, "Wake Not the Dead" Walter divorces his wife because he wants to reunite with his deceased first wife, which leaves his children exposed to danger; in Hildebrandt's novel, Alfred leaves his family for an extended period of time to try to mend his sister's marriage, which is heading toward divorce. When he leaves, Lodoiska arrives, and

Alfred's family is in danger because he is not there to protect them. In both stories, a weakened family unit, whether through the death of a child's parents, divorce, or the mere absence of the father, is ultimately destroyed by a female intruder who replaces the deceased mother. The archetypal stepmother from the Grimms' fairy tales has a new face now, and she has a whole new way of killing.

When the vampire from central European folklore was introduced to readers as a literary figure in the mid-eighteenth century and as a woman not long thereafter, it was immediately eroticized and became the focus of moralizing stories about defining gender roles and the family within the parameters of a strict moral code at the turn of the nineteenth century. At the end of the introduction to his book, *Monster Theory: Reading Culture*, Jeffrey Jerome Cohen suggests that "monsters ask us how we perceive the world, and how we have misrepresented what we have attempted to place. They ask us to reevaluate our assumptions about race, gender, sexuality, our perception of difference, our tolerance toward its expression. They ask us why we have created them" (Cohen 1996, 25). The vampires in these stories by Raupach and Hildebrandt ask us these questions, but they do more than that—they destabilize the images of women in literature, and challenge the reader's perception of the very real problem of infanticide in society.

KARL ADOLF VON WACHSMANN: "DER FREMDE" (THE MYSTERIOUS STRANGER; 1847)

The story of a man from western Europe traveling through a mountainous wooded landscape in eastern Europe to close a real estate transaction, only to run into a little trouble with a local vampire of noble lineage, is all too familiar to readers of vampire fiction. But this man is not Jonathan Harker, the vampire is not Count Dracula, and the author is not Bram Stoker. From May to June 1847, the German author Karl Adolf von Wachsmann published the story, "The Mysterious Stranger," in several installments in issues 56–76 of the German popular literary magazine, *Würzburger Conversationsblatt* (Würzburg Conversation Journal). This story was first published in English in *Chambers's Repository of Instructive and Amusing Tracts* in 1854, and six years later it was reprinted in the magazine, *Odds and Ends*.

In many ways, from the setting of the story to the image of the vampire, and especially the theme of real estate transaction, Wachsmann's story is a notable precursor to Bram Stoker's novel *Dracula* (written fifty years after "The Mysterious Stranger"). In fact, Leonard Wolf claims that there is little mistaking Bram Stoker's "inspired borrowing" in the book, *The Annotated Dracula* (1975), and John Edgar Browning identifies "numerous theatrical and film adaptations of *Dracula* [that] have bolstered more direct references to this story [by Wachsmann]" in his entry, "The Mysterious Stranger," in the *Encyclopedia of the Vampire: The Living Dead in Myth, Legend and Popular Culture* (2011, 215). In some instances, for example, in John Badham's 1979 film *Dracula,* lines are lifted word for word: Azzo, the vampire in our story by Wachsmann (Dracula, played by Frank Langella in the film), says to Franziska (Lucy, played by Kate Nelligan): "If my company does not please you at any time, you will have yourself to blame for an acquaintance with one who seldom forces himself, but is difficult to shake off."

Karl Adolf von Wachsmann was born in 1787 in Grünberg, Silesia (then part of the Holy Roman Empire of the German Nation) as the son of a retired cavalry captain. After serving in the Prussian military, Wachsmann became interested in pursuing literary interests and wrote for numerous popular magazines and journals. He became a very well-known and prolific author of novellas, publishing ninety-three novellas in thirty-seven volumes of his collection, *Erzählungen und Novellen* (Short Stories and Novellas), by 1849. His stories and novellas were very well received by the reading public, and critically acclaimed by one of the foremost contemporary German critics, Karl Goedeke.

This story is about Baron von Fahnenberg from Austria who is traveling with his family to claim a castle he inherited from a recently deceased childless brother in the mountains of Carniola, part of present-day Slovenia just east of Trieste, Italy. The original translator of the story (and subsequent translations) erroneously places the setting in the Carpathian Mountains, which are much farther east, stretching in a northwestern to southeastern arc through parts of Slovakia, southern Poland, Hungary, southwestern Ukraine, and Romania. As the family travels through these forests during a snowstorm with a local guide who knows of the dangers that lurk in the woods, they meet a mysterious stranger who has an uncanny control over the wolves who threaten the travelers on their journey. Calling himself Azzo von Klatka, the strange man is approximately forty years old, tall, thin, and very pale, and described by Fahnenberg's niece, Bertha, as corpse-like, dried up, and old-fashioned in dress. Throughout the story he is referred to repeatedly as the stranger and the unknown. In German, the term *der Fremde* (the stranger; also the original German title) is ambiguous, meaning both "the stranger" and "the foreigner."

After the family invites this stranger to visit them as a way of thanking him from keeping the wolves from attacking them, Baron von Fahnenberg's daughter, Franziska, falls victim to a strange illness that causes her to have nightmares of Azzo von Klatka coming into her room in the form of mist, and symptoms including sudden extreme weight loss, a deathly pallor, and a wound on her neck that will not heal. As her life energy is depleted, Azzo von Klatka's is replenished. It is not until a friend of the family, cousin Bertha's fiancé, Woislaw, arrives that Franziska can be saved. As his name implies, Woislaw has connections with eastern Europe. He is a knight from Silesia (then a German territory) who is fighting with the Habsburgs against the Ottoman Empire in one of the many wars between the Ottoman Empire and Austria, Venice, and Wallachia, which took place between 1593 and 1669. Since the setting is given as the "early seventeenth century," it is very likely the Long War (1591–1606) from which Woislaw returns. Also known as the Thirteen Years' War or the Fifteen Years' War, depending on whether you count it as beginning in 1591 or 1593, this war was a border conflict between the Habsburg monarchy and the Ottoman Empire over Balkan territories. Major participants were the Habsburg monarchy, the Principality of Transylvania, Wallachia, and Moldavia versus the Ottoman Empire.

Much like Van Helsing in Stoker's *Dracula*, the knight Woislaw is initially very secretive about his knowledge of vampires when he sets out to save Franziska's life, because he needs Franziska's full participation and devotion to a clearly defined ritual that she alone must perform in order to kill the vampire and heal herself, devoid of any doubt or skepticism that could occur if Woislaw even mentioned the word "vampire" to her. Much like Van Helsing, he acts immediately and methodically when he prepares the ritual, which involves staking Azzo's coffin with nails before he awakens. In Stoker's novel, Van Helsing is an intellectual match for Dracula, and his knowledge of vampire lore makes it possible for Mina, Jonathan, Dr. Seward, and Quincey Morris to defeat the vampire by driving him out of England and back to Transylvania. Similarly, Woislaw is a formidable opponent for the vampire Azzo, but not only due to his thorough knowledge of and experience with eastern European vampires; he also has superhuman strength, because he lost his arm in war and now has a gold prosthetic arm. Woislaw is a dangerous opponent for the vampire because of his combined cultural knowledge and physical strength. In fact, the vampire Azzo believes that Woislaw is a "blood-brother" when Woislaw grasps Azzo's hand in an effort to save Franziska's cousin (and future husband) Franz from Azzo.

The vampire Azzo lives in the ruins of Castle Klatka, which is on Fahnenberg's estate grounds, so it now belongs to Fahnenberg. Azzo acknowledges this transfer of property rights when he contemptuously answers Baron von Fahnenberg's question, "Do you live in these ruins?" as follows: "Yes; but not to the destruction of your game as you may fear, [Baron] von Fahnenberg. [. . .] Be quite assured of this; your property shall remain untouched." Of course, Klatka will not poach the new estate owner's game, but it is significant that his home, the ruins of the Castle Klatka, is on Fahnenberg's estate and Fahnenberg finds "the estate and affairs in greater disorder than he at first imagined; and instead of remaining three or four weeks, as was originally intended, their departure was deferred to an indefinite period." In an age of colonialism, the Fahnenberg family from Upper Austria (i.e., Habsburgs) are compelled not only to take possession of these lands in eastern

Europe, but also to improve them and bring this land that is described repeatedly as old-fashioned, quaint, and romantic up to Western—Austrian—standards.

When the Habsburgs acquired territories in eastern Europe from their many wars against the Ottoman Empire, they also acquired cultures that were very foreign to them. This interaction with a new culture was something Habsburg Emperor Charles VI took very seriously after his conquests in the early eighteenth century, so much so that he commissioned scientists to study the cultures of these new areas and especially their superstitions. Moreover, the image of the aristocratic vampire in nineteenth-century literature who lives in castle ruins or at the very least in castles in dire need of repair, though clearly magnificent in earlier times, can be understood as social commentary about a dying, (un)dead social class in the modern and changing nineteenth century. It is important to remember that this story was written in 1847, one year before the failed German revolution that sought to form a German nation under democratic principles. There was much criticism at the time of the state of Germany with its numerous principalities. Interestingly, literary vampires became aristocratic during the first half of the nineteenth century, suggesting that this social class was considered to be the walking dead. Powerful and dangerous? Yes, but more importantly, part of a bygone age, no longer relevant for the present or the future, but merely hanging onto existence, and of course, sucking the life force of its people.

The vampire knight Azzo von Klatka, for example, is a fine example of a metaphor for a social class that is crumbling to dust and can only be recognized as part of European history, not modernity. Though this social class is essentially dead in these modern times, remarkably it still wields power. But the criticism of Azzo's dying class is much harsher in this story than is Dracula's dying, though formerly noble and respectable family history. Azzo is described as "the last owner of the castle, which at the time was a sort of robbers' den and the headquarters of all depredators in the neighborhood [and as a man who] was feared not only on account of his passionate temper, but of his treaties with Turkish hordes." And of course, he carried off young women from the surrounding villages to a tower in his castle and they were never heard from again. He is not only the last of his line, but that noble line was corrupt, and worse, it produced criminals of the basest sort. Despite an uprising by peasants who were able to besiege his stronghold and kill him, he lives on. His home is in the ruins of his castle, and this is a comfortable enough existence for him. But it is not until the Fahnenbergs take possession of these lands (his home) where old-world aristocracy and superstition still exist, and improve on the state of life there, that this wild and romantic country can be raised to Western standards. The threat of a dying social class can thus be eradicated, and a western European concept of civilization can take hold.

NOTES

1. See chapter 1.
2. See chapter 1 for more information on this report of vampirism by Ranft.
3. See chapter 1.
4. The likely source for this scene and Hyppolit's discovery of his wife's cannibalism is "The Story Sîdi Nu'mâns and His Mare" from the fairy-tale collection, *One Thousand and One Nights*, with which Hoffmann was familiar (Segebrecht and Segebrecht 2001, 1634).
5. This story should not be confused with the play "Laßt die Todten ruhen," which Raupach published in 1826. The play does not address the vampire theme.
6. In his 1998 book, *The Monster with a Thousand Faces: Guises of the Vampire in Myth and Literature*, Brian J. Frost attributes "Wake Not the Dead" to Ludwig Tieck and claims that Charles Collins "rescued [the story] from obscurity" (38) in his anthology, *A Feast of Blood* (1967), but I have not been able to verify Collins's anthology as a source for "Wake Not the Dead," nor do any of the critical editions on Gothic literature or the vampire in literature cite Collins's anthology. The most widely referenced contemporary source for the story is Haining's anthology from 1972.
7. See, for example, Goethe's remarks about the Romantic "Nacht- und Grabdichter" in chapter 2.
8. See chapter 1.
9. See chapter 2.
10. See appendix.

Chapter Four

The Development of a Horror Aesthetic by German Poets

If the previous chapters have shown that the literary vampire, with its origins in German poetry and prose, was inspired by stories of the central European vampire superstition collected for Charles VI, and that the vampires created by German poets addresses social fears, taboos, and anxieties, then this study has been successful. These are the origins of the vampire in literature, but the following question remains: what impact did the German literary vampire from the eighteenth and early nineteenth centuries have on the future development of Gothic horror literature in general, and the development of the literary vampire specifically? It cannot be denied that German poets embellished the vampire from central European folklore and superstition with numerous traits that persist into the twenty-first century. The very first vampire poem, "The Vampire," by Heinrich August Ossenfelder, introduced the eroticization of death in connection with the vampire figure. German poets took a monster from folklore and superstition and projected onto it a combination of human fears, anxieties, taboos, and passions which, combined, come together to create a mosaic of opposing emotions. In the image of the vampire lover, there is also a fear of the unknown or even the termination of the life one had led previously. In addition to the theme of the eroticization of death that became programmatic for the literary vampire in the nineteenth and twentieth centuries and has continued in film, German poets introduced other innovative ideas in conjunction with the vampire figure, such as social and political commentary. E. T. A. Hoffmann in particular successfully combined numerous social taboos in a composite of the figures of the Baroness and her daughter, Aurelie, in his story "Vampirismus," connecting images of moral corruption with a noble social class as the embodiment of evil that sustains itself by preying on weaker individuals in a desperate attempt to continue its existence. The vampire embodies opposing passions that are reflective of the human condition, and the concentration of such strong, contrasting emotions in one horrific body creates an atmosphere of sublime horror in the earliest vampire poetry and prose.

TOWARD AN AESTHETIC OF HORROR

In the preface to his book, *Ästhetik des Horrors* (An Aesthetic of Horror) Hans Richard Brittnacher asks why authors and readers since the eighteenth century have been so interested in fantastical motifs, ghosts, vampires, monsters, devils, and automatons (Brittnacher 1994, 7). Moreover, Brittnacher observes that fantastic literature, especially horror literature, was and still is frowned upon in Germany, in stark contrast to its reception in Britain and France, for example (10). In fact, the German poets, composers, and filmmakers who have worked with this theme were very innovative and have greatly influenced the British and American authors of Gothic fiction who followed their lead, but there has been a simultaneous skepticism about its value as a subject for serious art.

In his book, *The Sublime* (1960), Samuel Monk addresses the intense interest among authors, poets, and theorists of the eighteenth century to explain how terror and horror could play such an important role in contemporary literature. Monk comes to the conclusion that the sublime, "an aesthetic effect resulting from the presentation of terrifying objects within some artistic form or from the contemplation of the awesome in a landscape" (quoted in Heller 1987, 201), could explain the appeal of horror literature, especially toward the end of the eighteenth century.

The oppositional valuation of horror literature between Germany and Britain can be explained in part when one considers that Edmund Burke's 1757 work, *Philosophical Enquiry about Our Origins of the Sublime and the Beautiful*, ultimately became programmatic for the development of Gothic horror fiction in Britain, making it possible for themes such as violence, pain, and death to attain aesthetic dignity (Burke 1998, 11–12). In his *Philosophical Enquiry* Burke relates terror to the sublime, suggesting that the experience of the sublime is characterized by astonishment: "that state of the soul in which all its motions are suspended with some degree of horror" (quoted in Heller 1987, 201). The experience of the sublime is quiet and awestruck. It is important to be aware at this point that aesthetic distance was crucial to the effect of the sublime, according to Burke.

Such a programmatic text for Gothic literature as Burke's was for Britain was not available to German authors of the fantastic in the late eighteenth century; instead, the aesthetic theory of the sublime in Germany at this time demanded the retraction of the horrific into the awareness of moral unassailability. Brittnacher sums this up as follows: "Laokoon durfte seufzen, aber nicht schreien, und auch seufzen nur gedämpft, in fünfhebigen Jamben" "Laokoon was allowed to moan, but not scream, and he was also only allowed to moan in a subdued manner, in iambic pentameter." (1994, 12). This has its roots in the German aesthetic tradition that began as a philosophical discipline with Immanuel Kant's *Critique of Judgment* (1790). Though Burke had laid the foundation for a theory of the sublime in 1757, as Samuel Monk points out, the concept of the sublime had not been adequately described in the eighteenth century until Kant published his third *Critique*. In an effort to clarify what constitutes the sublime, Kant paints a scene of

> boldly overhanging and, as it were, threatening rocks, thunderclouds piled up in the sky, moving along with thunder and lightning, volcanoes in all their destructive power, hurricanes with the destruction in their track, the boundless ocean rising in anger, a high cataract of a mighty river and so on. (quoted in Heller 1987, *Critique* §28)

However, actual sublimity cannot be achieved until the observer is aware of his or her independence or safe distance from and superiority over nature. Monk elaborates on Kant's theory of the sublime when he states:

> To be dynamically sublime, nature must be a source of fear, but not at the moment of aesthetic judgment. [. . .] If we are safe from [the] menace [of overhanging rocks, thunderclouds, volcanoes, etc. that Kant refers to] they become delightful because of their fearfulness. (quoted in Heller 1987, 203)

Hence, an experience of the sublime when confronted with fearful objects can only be achieved at an aesthetic distance to those objects. In *The Delights of Terror*, Terry Heller remarks: "Perhaps the potential for pleasure inherent in the tale of terror is fully articulated in the aesthetic effect of the sublime. If this is true, then it may also be true that all tales of terror seek in various ways to produce this effect" (1987, 206). As Heller points out, Kant replaces Burke's early description of the sublime as "stillness of astonishment," a quiet sense of awe, with "a mind in motion, specifically between attraction and repulsion" (204). The common dialectic of erotic attraction and sublime terror that was introduced by German poets in the early vampire ballads and prose works would become a universal theme that readers of Gothic fiction since the eighteenth century and horror film fans since the early twentieth century have simply come to expect. In their poems, Ossenfelder, Bürger, Goethe, and Eichendorff represent this emotion that alternates between attraction and repulsion, as do Tieck, Hoffmann, and Raupach in their prose works, varying only in methods and skill. On the one hand, we are attracted by the beauty of the poetic form in a ballad, such as Goethe's "The Bride of Corinth" and the initial idealistic beauty of the bride's appearance and demeanor before the witching hour strikes, only to be repulsed when her true nature bursts forth at the end of the poem in all its wanton passion and brutality. We pity Lenore's tragic loss of her fiancé, only to be horrified at her punishment for renouncing God in her despair over the loss of her lover. In Eichendorff's poems we experience the attraction and then the horror that the lovers are subjected to when they become aware of their lovers' true identities.

This erotic attraction/repulsion dialectic continues in the prose works by Tieck, Hoffmann, Raupach, and Wachsmann though Raupach leaves no room for pity or compassion for Walter, who knowingly desires intercourse with a reanimated corpse. In "Wake Not the Dead," we are not only repulsed by the vampire lover, Brunhilde, but maybe even more so by Walter, who made it possible for her to terrorize the surrounding villages and his own children, stopping her only when she threatened him. The common theme of erotic attraction and repulsion in these early vampire works is representative of the larger Gothic theme of uncertainty that results in fear and suspicion. The erotic element and the intimacy between lovers in these poems and stories intensify the fear that is associated with feelings of uncertainty, because of the profound level of trust that one expects to find between lovers. The tragedy that results from betrayal and murder is naturally more intense, the more intimately entwined the two characters are. Moreover, when one of these poems or stories remains open, with the fate of the vampire or the lover hanging in the balance, the reader experiences Gothic dread at the possibility that the limitless terror this vampire bride represents is eternal. The effect is one of sublime aesthetic horror.

INTERNATIONAL IMPACT

The broad international influence that eighteenth- and nineteenth-century German poets had on authors of horror fiction, especially in Great Britain and America, is well known. Edgar Allan Poe, for example, was very fond of the works of Ludwig Tieck and E. T. A. Hoffmann, and this is evident in his writing. He was also very likely inspired by the English translation of Ernst Benjamin Salomo Raupach's story, "Wake Not the Dead," because he deals equally well with the conflict between morality and passion; the theme of a woman's beauty in death became particularly common in Poe's work.

In fact, German Gothic horror fiction was so popular in Britain that Gothic writers often included the words "A German Story" or the equivalent as a subtitle in order to give their novels better credibility as sufficiently and quite pleasingly horrid. The positive reception of Raupach's story, for example, especially among contemporary British readers, is not surprising in light of the great interest British readers had in Gothic horror literature from Germany, or at least set in Germany, since the 1790s that continued into the nineteenth century. Jane Austen satirizes what she viewed as an indiscriminate Gothic literature craze in her novel, *Northanger Abbey*, published posthumously by Austen's brother in 1818. In the novel, Isabella recommends several Gothic tales to her friend, Catherine, many of which are originally German or set in Germany:

> and when you have finished Udolpho, we will read the Italian together; and I have made out a list of ten or twelve more of the same kind for you [. . .] I will read you their names directly; here they are, in my pocketbook. Castle of Wolfenbach, Clermont, Mysterious Warnings, Necromancer of the Black Forest, Midnight Bell, Orphan of the Rhine, and Horrid Mysteries. Those will last us some time. (Austen 1995, 39)[1]

In response, Catherine asks the most important and relevant question for an interested reader of Gothic horror fiction at the time: "Yes, pretty well; but are they all horrid, are you sure they are all horrid?" Isabella assures her that they are indeed horrid. Raupach's story is horrid and might have been mentioned with the others if it had been written earlier. Nevertheless, the positive reception of Raupach's story in Britain is evident in its immediate translation into English and its inclusion soon after in two multivolume anthologies of Gothic horror literature that have been widely referenced among scholars of Gothic horror literature until the present day.

Despite the great influence that German poets had on British and American authors of Gothic horror fiction, and the variety of specific motifs and characteristics that German poets brought to the image of the vampire, their conceptions of Gothic horror diverged somewhat from the pattern set by British and American authors in the nineteenth century. A common characteristic of some of the greatest works of Gothic fiction by eighteenth- and nineteenth-century British authors in particular is that the events and the apparent convergence of supernatural forces that come together in the narrative to create an atmosphere of mystery are ultimately explained rationally. As we have seen in the poems and prose works discussed here, the German poets do not offer rational explanations for the observed phenomena, nor do they provide solutions for the protagonists. In the poems, the vampires' victims die, or this is at least implied, but there is no rational explanation for the events that are described. In Goethe's poem, the bride lets her mother know how to put an end to her cursed existence as a vampire, but the reader is left wondering whether or not she was killed. In the prose works the victims are either killed, or they go insane. The effect of this "unexplained horror" that is common in the first vampire literature by German authors is that this horror will continue. Indeed, the vampire never dies.

NOTE

1. Eliza Parsons, *The Castle of Wolfenbach, A German Story* (2 vols., London, 1793) and *The Mysterious Warning, A German Tale* (4 vols., London, 1796); Regina Maria Roche, *Clermont, A Tale* (4 vols., 1798); Peter Teuthold, *The Necromancer, or the Tale of the Black Forest* (2 vols., London, 1794, translated from the German of L. Flammenberg); Francis Lathom, *The Midnight Bell, A German Story* (3 vols., London: printed for H. D. Symonds, 1798); Eleanor Sleath, *The Orphan of the Rhine, a Romance* (4 vols., London, 1798); Peter Will, *Horrid Mysteries: A Story* (4 vols., 1796, from the German of the Marquis of Grosse) (Austen 247). Since the publication of this edition of Jane Austen's novel, it has been established by James D. Jenkins that the novel attributed to Peter Teuthold in the list of so-called "Northanger novels" above is actually the translation of *Der Geisterbanner: Eine Wundergeschichte aus mündlichen und schriftlichen Traditionen gesammelt*, "published by Johann Baptist Wallishauser at Hohenzollern in 1792 and attributed to 'Lorenz Flammenberg.' Lorenz . . . Flammenberg was in fact a pseudonym for Karl Friedrich Kahlert (1765–1813)" (Jenkins 2007, ix).

Appendix

Vampire Poems

HEINRICH AUGUST OSSENFELDER (1725–1801): "THE VAMPIRE" (1748)

My dear young maiden clingeth
Unbending, fast and firm
To all the long-held teachings
Of an ever-faithful mother;
As folk along the Theyse
Heyduck-like do believe
In vampires that bring death.
But my dear Christiana, just wait,
Thou dost not want to love me;
I will myself avenge
And today in Tockay
Drink thee to a vampire.
And as softly thou art sleeping
From thy lovely cheeks
Will suck fresh crimson color.
And so shalt thou be startled
When I kiss thee thus
And as a vampire kiss:
When then thou dost truly tremble
And limply in my arms
Dost sink like one dead,
Then shall I thee question
Are my teachings not better
Than those of thy good mother?

GOTTFRIED AUGUST BÜRGER (1747–1794): "LENORE" (1774)

Up rose Lenore as the red morn wore,
From weary visions starting;
"Art faithless, William, or, William, art dead?
'Tis long since thy departing."
For he, with Frederick's men of might,
In fair Prague waged the uncertain fight;
Nor once had he writ in the hurry of war,
And sad was the true heart that sickened afar.

The Empress and the King,
With ceaseless quarrel tired,
At length relaxed the stubborn hate
Which rivalry inspired:
And the martial throng, with laugh and song,
Spoke of their homes as they rode along,
And clank, clank, clank! came every rank,
With the trumpet-sound that rose and sank.

And here and there and everywhere,
Along the swarming ways,
Went old man and boy, with music of joy,
On the gallant bands to gaze;
And the young child shouted to spy the vaward,
And trembling and blushing the bride pressed forward:
But ah! for the sweet lips of Lenore
The kiss and the greeting are vanished and o'er.

From man to man all wildly she ran
With a swift and searching eye;
But she felt alone in the mighty mass,
As it crushed and crowded by:
On hurried the troop,—a gladsome group,—
And proudly the tall plumes wave and droop:
She tore her hair and she turned her round,
And madly she dashed her against the ground.

Her mother clasped her tenderly
With soothing words and mild:
"My child, may God look down on thee,—
God comfort thee, my child."
"Oh! mother, mother! gone is gone!
I reck no more how the world runs on:
What pity to me does God impart?
Woe, woe, woe! for my heavy heart!"

"Help, Heaven, help and favour her!

Child, utter an Ave Marie!
Wise and great are the doings of God;
He loves and pities thee."
"Out, mother, out, on the empty lie!
Doth he heed my despair,—doth he list to my cry?
What boots it now to hope or to pray?
The night is come,—there is no more day."

"Help, Heaven, help! who knows the Father
Knows surely that he loves his child:
The bread and the wine from the hand divine
Shall make thy tempered grief less wild."
"Oh! mother, dear mother! the wine and the bread
Will not soften the anguish that bows down my head;
For bread and for wine it will yet be as late
That his cold corpse creeps from the grim grave's gate."

"What if the traitor's false faith failed,
By sweet temptation tried,—
What if in distant Hungary
He clasp another bride?—
Despise the fickle fool, my girl,
Who hath ta'en the pebble and spurned the pearl:
While soul and body shall hold together
In his perjured heart shall be stormy weather."

"Oh! mother, mother! gone is gone,
And lost will still be lost!
Death, death is the goal of my weary soul,
Crushed and broken and crost.
Spark of my life! down, down to the tomb:
Die away in the night, die away in the gloom!
What pity to me does God impart?
Woe, woe, woe! for my heavy heart!"

"Help, Heaven, help, and heed her not,
For her sorrows are strong within;
She knows not the words that her tongue repeats,—
Oh! Count them not for sin!
Cease, cease, my child, thy wretchedness,
And think on the promised happiness;
So shall thy mind's calm ecstasy
Be a hope and a home and a bridegroom to thee."

"My mother, what is happiness?
My mother, what is Hell?
With William is my happiness,—
Without him is my Hell!

Spark of my life! down, down to the tomb:
Die away in the night, die away in the gloom!
Earth and Heaven, Heaven and earth,
Reft of William are nothing worth."

Thus grief racked and tore the breast of Lenore,
And was busy at her brain;
Thus rose her cry to the Power on high,
To question and arraign:
Wringing her hands and beating her breast,—
Tossing and rocking without any rest;—
Till from her light veil the moon shone thro',
And the stars leapt out on the darkling blue.

But hark to the clatter and the pat pat patter!
Of a horse's heavy hoof!
How the steel clanks and rings as the rider springs!
How the echo shouts aloof!
While silently and lightly the gentle bell
Tingles and jingles softly and well;
And low and clear through the door plank thin
Comes the voice without to the ear within:

"Holla! holla! unlock the gate;
Art waking, my bride, or sleeping?
Is thy heart still free and faithful to me?
Art laughing, my bride, or weeping?"
"Oh! wearily, William, I've waited for you,—
Woefully watching the long day thro',—
With a great sorrow sorrowing
For the cruelty of your tarrying."

"Till the dead midnight we saddled not,
I have journeyed far and fast—
And hither I come to carry thee back
Ere the darkness shall be past."
"Ah! rest thee within till the night's more calm;
Smooth shall thy couch be, and soft, and warm:
Hark to winds, how they whistle and rush
Thro' the twisted twine of the hawthorn-bush."

"Thro' the hawthorn-bush let whistle and rush,—
Let whistle, child, let whistle!
Mark the flash fierce and high of my steed's bright eye,
And his proud crest's eager bristle.
Up, up and away! I must not stay:
Mount swiftly behind me! up, up and away!
An hundred miles must be ridden and sped

Ere we may lie down in the bridal-bed."

"What! ride an hundred miles to-night,
By thy mad fancies driven!
Dost hear the bell with its sullen swell,
As it rumbles out eleven?"
"Look forth! look forth! the moon shines bright:
We and the dead gallop fast thro' the night.
'Tis for a wager I bear thee away
To the nuptial couch ere break of day."

"Ah! where is the chamber, William dear,
And William, where is the bed?"
"Far, far from here: still, narrow, and cool:
Plank and bottom and lid."
"Hast room for me?"—"For me and thee;
Up, up to the saddle right speedily!
The wedding-guests are gathered and met,
And the door of the chamber is open set."

She busked her well, and into the selle
She sprang with nimble haste,—
And gently smiling, with a sweet beguiling,
Her white hands clasped his waist:—
And hurry, hurry! ring, ring, ring!
To and fro they sway and swing;
Snorting and snuffing they skim the ground,
And the sparks fly up, and the stones run round.

Here to the right and there to the left
Flew fields of corn and clover,
And the bridges flashed by to the dazzled eye,
As rattling they thundered over.
"What ails my love? the moon shines bright:
Bravely the dead men ride through the night.
Is my love afraid of the quiet dead?"
"Ah! no;—let them sleep in their dusty bed!"

On the breeze cool and soft what tune floats aloft,
While the crows wheel overhead?—
Ding dong! ding dong! 'tis the sound, 'tis the song,—
"Room, room for the passing dead!"
Slowly the funeral-train drew near,
Bearing the coffin, bearing the bier;
And the chime of their chant was hissing and harsh,
Like the note of the bull-frog within the marsh.

"You bury your corpse at the dark midnight,

With hymns and bells and wailing;—
But I bring home my youthful wife
To a bride-feast's rich regaling.
Come, chorister, come with thy choral throng,
And solemnly sing me a marriage-song;
Come, friar, come,— let the blessing be spoken,
That the bride and the bridegroom's sweet rest be unbroken."

Died the dirge and vanished the bier:—
Obedient to his call,
Hard hard behind, with a rush like the wind,
Came the long steps' pattering fall:
And ever further! ring, ring, ring!
To and fro they sway and swing;
Snorting and snuffing they skim the ground,
And the sparks spurt up, and the stones run round.

How flew to the right, how flew to the left,
Trees, mountains in the race!
How to the left, and the right and the left,
Flew town and market-place!
"What ails my love? the moon shines bright:
Bravely the dead men ride thro' the night.
Is my love afraid of the quiet dead?"
"Ah! let them alone in their dusty bed!"

See, see, see! by the gallows-tree,
As they dance on the wheel's broad hoop,
Up and down, in the gleam of the moon
Half lost, an airy group:—
"Ho, ho! mad mob, come hither amain,
And join in the wake of my rushing train;—
Come, dance me a dance, ye dancers thin,
Ere the planks of the marriage bed close us in."

And hush, hush, hush! the dreamy rout
Came close with a ghastly bustle,
Like the whirlwind in the hazel-bush,
When it makes the dry leaves rustle:
And faster, faster! ring, ring, ring!
To and fro they sway and swing;
Snorting and snuffing they skim the ground,
And the sparks spurt up, and the stones run round.

How flew the moon high overhead,
In the wild race madly driven!
In and out, how the stars danced about,
And reeled o'er the flashing heaven!

Appendix 115

"What ails my love? the moon shines bright:
Bravely the dead men ride thro' the night.
Is my love afraid of the quiet dead?"
"Alas! let them alone in their dusty bed!"

"Horse, horse! meseems 'tis the cock's shrill note,
And the sand is well nigh spent;
Horse, horse, away! 'tis the break of day,—
'Tis the morning air's sweet scent.
Finished, finished is our ride:
Room, room for the bridegroom and the bride!
At last, at last, we have reached the spot,
For the speed of the dead man has slackened not!"

And swiftly up to an iron gate
With reins relaxed they went;
At the rider's touch the bolts flew back,
And the bars were broken and bent;
The doors were burst with a deafening knell,
And over the white graves they dashed pell mell:
The tombs around looked grassy and grim,
As they glimmered and glanced in the moonlight dim.

But see! But see! in an eyelid's beat,
Towhoo! a ghastly wonder!
The horseman's jerkin, piece by piece,
Dropped off like brittle tinder!
Fleshless and hairless, a naked skull,
The sight of his weird head was horrible;
The lifelike mask was there no more,
And a scythe and a sandglass the skeleton bore.

Loud snorted the horse as he plunged and reared,
And the sparks were scattered round:—
What man shall say if he vanished away,
Or sank in the gaping ground?
Groans from the earth and shrieks in the air!
Howling and wailing everywhere!
Half dead, half living, the soul of Lenore
Fought as it never had fought before.

The churchyard troop,—a ghostly group,—
Close round the dying girl;
Out and in they hurry and spin
Through the dancer's weary whirl:
"Patience, patience, when the heart is breaking;
With thy God there is no question-making:
Of thy body thou art quit and free:

Heaven keep thy soul eternally!"

JOHANN WOLFGANG VON GOETHE (1749–1832): "THE BRIDE OF CORINTH" (1797)

Once a stranger youth to Corinth came,
Who in Athens lived, but hoped that he
From a certain townsman there might claim,
As his father's friend, kind courtesy.
Son and daughter, they
Had been wont to say
Should thereafter bride and bridegroom be.

But can he that boon so highly prized,
Save 'tis dearly bought, now hope to get?
They are Christians and have been baptized,
He and all of his are heathens yet.
For a newborn creed,
Like some loathsome weed,
Love and truth to root out oft will threat.

Father, daughter, all had gone to rest,
And the mother only watches late;
She receives with courtesy the guest,
And conducts him to the room of state.
Wine and food are brought,
Ere by him besought
Bidding him good night, she leaves him straight.

But he feels no relish now, in truth,
For the dainties so profusely spread;
Meat and drink forgets the wearied youth,
And, still dress'd, he lays him on the bed.
Scarce are closed his eyes,
When a form in-hies
Through the open door with silent tread.

By his glimmering lamp discerns he now
How, in veil and garment white array'd,
With a black and gold band round her brow,
Glides into the room a bashful maid.
But she, at his sight,
Lifts her hand so white,
And appears as though full sore afraid.

"Am I," cries she, "such a stranger here,
That the guest's approach they could not name?

Ah, they keep me in my cloister drear,
Well nigh feel I vanquish'd by my shame.
On thy soft couch now
Slumber calmly thou!
I'll return as swiftly as I came."

"Stay, thou fairest maiden!" cries the boy,
Starting from his couch with eager haste:
"Here are Ceres', Bacchus' gifts of joy;
Amor bringest thou, with beauty grac'd!
Thou art pale with fear!
Loved one let us here
Prove the raptures the Immortals taste."

"Draw not nigh, O Youth! afar remain!
Rapture now can never smile on me;
For the fatal step, alas! is ta'en,
Through my mother's sick-bed phantasy.
Cured, she made this oath:
'Youth and nature both
Shall henceforth to Heav'n devoted be.'

From the house, so silent now, are driven
All the gods who reign'd supreme of yore;
One Invisible now rules in heaven,
On the cross a Saviour they adore.
Victims slay they here,
Neither lamb nor steer,
But the altars reek with human gore."

And he lists, and ev'ry word he weighs,
While his eager soul drinks in each sound:
"Can it be that now before my gaze
Stands my loved one on this silent ground?
Pledge to me thy troth!
Through our father's oath:
With Heav'ns blessing will our love be crown'd."

"Kindly youth, I never can be thine!
'Tis my sister they intend for thee.
When I in the silent cloister pine,
Ah, within her arms remember me!
Thee alone I love,
While love's pangs I prove
Soon the earth will veil my misery."

"No! for by this glowing flame I swear,
Hymen hath himself propitious shown:

Let us to my fathers house repair,
And thoult find that joy is not yet flown,
Sweetest, here then stay,
And without delay
Hold we now our wedding feast alone!"

Then exchange they tokens of their truth;
She gives him a golden chain to wear,
And a silver chalice would the youth
Give her in return of beauty rare.
"That is not for me;
Yet I beg of thee,
One lock only give me of thy hair."

Now the ghostly hour of midnight knell'd,
And she seem'd right joyous at the sign;
To her pallid lips the cup she held,
But she drank of nought but blood-red wine.
For to taste the bread
There before them spread,
Nought he spoke could make the maid incline.

To the youth the goblet then she brought,—
He too quaff'd with eager joy the bowl.
Love to crown the silent feast he sought,
Ah! full love-sick was the stripling's soul.
From his prayer she shrinks,
Till at length he sinks
On the bed and weeps without control.

And she comes, and lays her near the boy:
"How I grieve to see thee sorrowing so!
If thou think'st to clasp my form with joy,
Thou must learn this secret sad to know;
Yes! the maid, whom thou
Call'st thy loved one now,
Is as cold as ice, though white as snow."

Then he clasps her madly in his arm,
While love's youthful might pervades his frame:
"Thou might'st hope, when with me, to grow warm.
E'en if from the grave thy spirit came!
Breath for breath, and kiss!
Overflow of bliss!
Dost not thou, like me, feel passion's flame?"

Love still closer rivets now their lips,
Tears they mingle with their rapture blest,

From his mouth the flame she wildly sips,
Each is with the other's thought possess'd.
His hot ardour's flood
Warms her chilly blood,
But no heart is beating in her breast.

In her care to see that nought went wrong,
Now the mother happen'd to draw near;
At the door long hearkens she, full long,
Wond'ring at the sounds that greet her ear.
Tones of joy and sadness,
And love's blissful madness,
As of bride and bridegroom they appear.

From the door she will not now remove
Till she gains full certainty of this;
And with anger hears she vows of love,
Soft caressing words of mutual bliss.
"Hush! the cock's loud strain!
But thoult come again,
When the night returns!"—then kiss on kiss.

Then her wrath the mother cannot hold,
But unfastens straight the lock with ease
"In this house are girls become so bold,
As to seek e'en strangers' lusts to please?"
By her lamp's clear glow
Looks she in,—and oh!
Sight of horror!—'tis her child she sees.

Fain the youth would, in his first alarm,
With the veil that o'er her had been spread,
With the carpet, shield his love from harm;
But she casts them from her, void of dread,
And with spirit's strength,
In its spectre length,
Lifts her figure slowly from the bed.

"Mother! mother!"—Thus her wan lips say:
"May not I one night of rapture share?
From the warm couch am I chased away?
Do I waken only to despair?
It contents not thee
To have driven me
An untimely shroud of death to wear?

"But from out my coffin's prison-bounds
By a wond'rous fate I'm forced to rove,

While the blessings and the chaunting sounds
That your priests delight in, useless prove.
Water, salt, are vain
Fervent youth to chain,
Ah, e'en Earth can never cool down love!

"When that infant vow of love was spoken,
Venus' radiant temple smiled on both.
Mother! thou that promise since hast broken,
Fetter'd by a strange, deceitful oath.
Gods, though, hearken ne'er,
Should a mother swear
To deny her daughter's plighted troth.

From my grave to wander I am forc'd,
Still to seek The Good's long-sever'd link,
Still to love the bridegroom I have lost,
And the life-blood of his heart to drink;
When his race is run,
I must hasten on,
And the young must 'neath my vengeance sink.

"Beauteous youth! no longer mayst thou live;
Here must shrivel up thy form so fair;
Did not I to thee a token give,
Taking in return this lock of hair?
View it to thy sorrow!
Grey thoult be to-morrow,
Only to grow brown again when there.

"Mother, to this final prayer give ear!
Let a funeral pile be straightway dress'd;
Open then my cell so sad and drear,
That the flames may give the lovers rest!
When ascends the fire
From the glowing pyre,
To the gods of old we'll hasten, blest."

Works Cited

Aarne, Antti. 1971. *The Types of the Folk-Tale: A Classification and Bibliography*. New York: Lenox Hill. First published in 1910.
Aguirre, Manuel. 1990. *The Closed Space: Horror Literature and Western Symbolism*. New York: St. Martin's Press.
Allen, Virginia M. 1983. *The Femme Fatale: Erotic Icon*. Troy, NY: The Whitston Publishing Company.
Ariès, Philippe. 1995. *Geschichte des Todes*. Trans. Hans-Horst Henschen and Una Pfau. Munich: Carl Hanser.
Auerbach, Nina. 1995. *Our Vampires, Ourselves*. Chicago: University of Chicago Press.
Austen, Jane. 1995. *Northanger Abbey*. London: Penguin Books. First published 1817.
Bächthold-Stäubli, Hanns, and E. Hoffmann-Krayer. 1927–1942."Nachzehrer." *Handwörterbuch des deutschen Aberglaubens*. 10 vols. Berlin: Walter de Gruyter.
Barber, Paul. 2010. *Vampires, Burial, and Death: Folklore and Reality*. New Haven, CT: Yale University Press.
Barkhoff, Jürgen. 2008. "Female Vampires, Victimhood, and Vengeance in German Literature around 1800." In *Women and Death: Representations of Female Victims and Perpetrators in German Culture 1500–2000*, edited by Helen Fronius, 128–43. Rochester, NY: Camden House.
Barnaby, Paul. n.d. "Biography" and "E-Texts." The Walter Scott Digital Archive, Edinburgh University Library. http://www.walterscott.lib.ed.ac.uk/.
Bartlett, W. B., and Flavia Idriceanu. 2008. *Legends of Blood: The Vampire in History and Myth*. Westport, CT: Praeger.
Best, Otto F. 1987. *Die deutsche Literatur in Text und Darstellung: Aufklärung und Rokoko*. Stuttgart: Reclam.
Beutler, Ernst. 1948–1971. *Johann Wolfgang von Goethe: Gedenkausgabe der Werke, Briefe und Gespräche*. 27 vols. Zürich: Artemis.
Bloom, Clive. 1998. *Gothic Horror: A Reader's Guide from Poe to King and Beyond*. New York: St. Martin's Press.
Brittnacher, Hans Richard. 1994. *Ästhetik des Horrors*. Frankfurt: Suhrkamp.
Brown, H. M. 2006. *E. T. A. Hoffmann and the Serapiontic Principle: Critique and Creativity*. Rochester, NY: Camden House.
Browning, John Edgar. 2011. "The Mysterious Stranger." In *Encyclopedia of the Vampire: The Living Dead in Myth, Legend and Popular Culture*, edited by S. T. Joshi, 215–16. Santa Barbara, CA: Greenwood Press.
Bunson, Matthew. 1993. *The Vampire Encyclopedia*. New York: Gramercy Books.

Burke, Edmund. 1998. *A Philosophical Enquiry into the Origin of Our Ideas of the Sublime and Beautiful*. Edited by David Womersley. New York: Penguin Books.
Burman, Edward. 1985. *The Inquisition: Hammer of Heresy*. New York: Dorset Press.
Carroll, Noël. 1990. *The Philosophy of Horror or Paradoxes of the Heart*. New York: Routledge.
Caswell, Pamela, and Sarah Webster Goodwin. 1988. "Death and the Individual." In *Dictionary of Literary Themes and Motifs*, edited by Jean-Charles Seigneuret, 328–45. Westport, CT: Greenwood Press.
Cohen, Jeffrey Jerome. 1996. *Monster Theory: Reading Culture*. Minneapolis: University of Minnesota Press.
Cornwell, Neil. 2000. "European Gothic." In *A Companion to the Gothic*, edited by David Punter, 27–38. Walden, MA: Blackwell Publishing.
Daemmrich, Horst S., and Ingrid Daemmrich. 1987. *Themes and Motifs in Western Literature: A Handbook*. Tübingen: Francke.
de Beauvoir, Simone. 1993. *The Second Sex*. London: David Campbell.
Frank, Manfred. 1985. *Ludwig Tieck: Schriften in zwölf Bänden*. Vol. 6. Frankfurt: Deutscher Klassiker Verlag.
Frayling, Christopher. 1991. *Vampyres: Lord Byron to Count Dracula*. London: Faber.
Frenzel, Elisabeth. 1966. *Stoff- und Motivgeschichte*. Berlin: Erich Schmidt.
———. 1988. *Motive der Weltliteratur: Ein Lexikon dichtungsgeschichtlicher Längsschnitte*. 3rd ed. Stuttgart: Kröner.
Fronius, Helen. 2008. *Women and Death: Representations of Female Victims and Perpetrators in German Culture 1500–2000*. Rochester, NY: Camden House.
Frost, Brian J. 1998. *The Monster with a Thousand Faces: Guises of the Vampire in Myth and Literature*. Bowling Green, OH: Bowling Green University Press.
Fulbrook, Mary. 2004. *A Concise History of Germany*. Cambridge: Cambridge University Press.
Goedeke, Karl. 1989. *Grundrisz zur Geschichte der deutschen Dichtung*. Vols. 1–18. Dresden: L. Ehlermann.
Graves, Robert. 1960. *The Greek Myths: Volume 1*. New York: Penguin Books.
Grimm, Gunter E. 1988. *Gedichte und Interpretationen: Deutsche Balladen*. Stuttgart: Reclam.
Haining, Peter. 1972. *Gothic Tales of Terror: Classic Horror Stories from Great Britain, Europe and the United States, 1765–1840*. New York: Taplinger.
Haller, Rudolf. 1962. *Eichendorffs Balladenwerk*. Munich: Francke.
Hammermeister, Kai. 2002. *The German Aesthetic Tradition*. Cambridge: Cambridge University Press.
Häntzschel, Günter, and Hiltrud Häntzschel. 1987. *Gottfried August Bürger: Sämtliche Werke*. Munich: Carl Hanser.
Heiske, Wilhelm, and Erich Seemann. 1967. *Deutsche Volkslieder mit ihren Melodien*. Vol. 5. Freiburg: Verlag des Deutschen Volksliedarchivs.
Heller, Terry. 1987. *The Delights of Terror: An Aesthetics of the Tale of Terror*. Urbana: University of Illinois Press.
Hillach, Ansgar and Klaus-Dieter Krabiel. 1972. *Eichendorff-Kommentar*. Munich: Winkler.
Hock, Stefan. 1900. *Die Vampyrsagen und ihre Verwertung in der deutschen Literatur*. Edited by Franz Muckner, 1977. Hildesheim: Gerstenberg Verlag.
Hoffmann, Friedrich G., and Herbert Rösch. 1984. *Grundlagen, Stile, Gestalten der deutschen Literatur: Eine geschichtliche Darstellung*. Frankfurt: Cornelsen.
Jenkins, James D. 2007. Preface to *The Necromancer; or The Tale of the Black Forest. Founded on Facts*. Translated from the German of Lawrence Flammenberg by Peter Teuthold. vi–xiv. Valancourt Books
Kaim-Kloock, Lore. 1963. *Gottfried August Bürger—Zum Problem der Volkstümlichkeit in der Lyrik*. Berlin: Rütten Loening.
Kaiser, Gerhard. 1976. *Aufklärung, Empfindsamkeit, Sturm und Drang*. Munich: Francke.
Karthaus, Ulrich. 1976. *Die deutsche Literatur in Text und Darstellung: Sturm und Drang und Empfindsamkeit*. Stuttgart: Reclam.

Klaniczay, Gábor. 1990. *The Uses of Supernatural Power: The Transformation of Popular Religion in Medieval and Early-Modern Europe*. Princeton, NJ: Princeton University Press.
Koepke, Wulf. 2000. *Die Deutschen: Vergangenheit und Gegenwart*. Orlando, FL: Harcourt, 2000.
Koopmann, Helmut. 1982. *Schillerforschung: 1970–1980. Ein Bericht*. Marbach am Neckar: Deutsche Schillergesellschaft.
———. 1998. *Schiller-Handbuch*. Stuttgart: Kröner.
Leavy, Barbara Fass. 1988. "La belle Dame sans merci." In *Dictionary of Literary Themes and Motifs*, edited by Jean-Charles Seigneuret, 169–74. Westport, CT: Greenwood Press, 1988.
Lewis, Paul. 1979. "The Intellectual Functions of Gothic Fiction: Poe's 'Ligeia' and Tieck's 'Wake Not the Dead.'" *Comparative Literature Studies* 16, no. 3 (Sept.): 207–21.
Lloyd-Smith, Allan. 2000. "Nineteenth-Century American Gothic." In *A Companion to the Gothic*, edited by David Punter, 109–21. Walden, MA: Blackwell Publishing.
Lüthi, Max. 1980. "Motif, Zug, Thema aus der Sicht der Volkserzählungsforschung." In *Elemente der Literatur*, edited by A. J. Bisanz and R. Trousson, 11–22. Stuttgart: Kröner.
Mamatey, Victor S. 1987. *The Rise of the Habsburg Empire 1526–1815*. Huntington, NY: Robert E. Krieger.
Marx, Karl. 1999. *Capital*. Edited by David McLellan. New York: Oxford University Press. First published 1867.
McNally, Raymond T. 1974. *A Clutch of Vampires*. Greenwich: New York Graphic Society.
McNally, Raymond, and Radu Florescu. 1994. *In Search of Dracula: The History of Dracula and Vampires*. New York: Houghton Mifflin.
Melton, J. Gordon. 1999. *The Vampire Book: The Encyclopedia of the Undead*. Farmington Hills, MI: Visible Ink Press.
Metzger, Lore. 1994. "Modification of Genre: A Feminist Critique of 'Christabel' and 'Die Braut von Korinth.'" In *Borderwork: Feminist Engagements with Comparative Literature*, edited by Margaret R. Higonnet, 81–99. Ithaca, NY: Cornell University Press.
Miller, Elizabeth. 2000. *Dracula: Sense and Nonsense*. Westcliff-on-Sea, UK: Desert Island Books.
Paulin, Roger. 1985. *Ludwig Tieck: A Literary Biography*. New York: Oxford University Press.
Perkowski, Jan Louis. 1976. *Vampires of the Slavs*. Cambridge, MA: Slavica Publishers.
Potter, Franz J. 2005. *The History of Gothic Publishing: Exhuming the Trade*. New York: Palgrave Macmillan.
Pufendorf, Samuel. 1667. *De statu imperii germanici liber unus*. Geneva: n.p.
Punter, David. 2000. *A Companion to the Gothic*. Walden, MA: Blackwell Publishing.
Raupach, Ernst Benjamin Salomo. 1823. *Laßt die Todten ruhen*. Leipzig: Gerhard Fleischer.
Schaeffer, John D. 1988. "Dialogue." In *Dictionary of Literary Themes and Motifs*, edited by Jean-Charles Seigneuret, 387. Westport, CT: Greenwood Press.
Schmidt, Erich. 1887. *Allgemeine Deutsche Biographie*. n.p.
Schmidt-Kaspar, Herbert. 1986. "Bürger's 'Lenore.'" In *Ballade*, edited by Christian Freitag, 220–31. Bamberg: C.C. Buchners.
Schöne, Albrecht. 1980. "Bürger's 'Lenore.'" In *Balladenforschung*, edited by Walter Müller-Seidel, 168–86. Meisenheim: Verlag Anton Hain.
Schroeder, Aribert. 1973. *Vampirismus: Seine Entwicklung vom Thema zum Motiv*. Frankfurt: Akademische Verlagsgesellschaft.
Scott, Walter. 1857. *The Poetical Works of Sir Walter Scott, With Memoir of the Author*. 9 Vols. Boston: Little, Brown & Co.
Segebrecht, Wulf, and Ursula Segebrecht. 2001. Vol. 4. *E. T. A. Hoffmann: Sämtliche Werke*. Frankfurt: Deutscher Klassiker Verlag.
Sherwood, Gilbert, and Piper, Paternoster Row. 1826. *Legends of Terror! And Tales of the Wonderful and the Wild. Original and Select, in Prose and Verse*. Edinburgh: Sherwood, Gilbert, and Piper, Paternoster Row.
Simpkin W. and R. Marshall. 1823. *Popular Tales and Romances of the Northern Nations*. Tavistock Street, London: Bohte.
Stoker, Bram. 1993. *Dracula*. New York: Penguin Books. First published 1897.
Stollberg-Rilinger, Barbara. 2000. *Europa im Jahrhundert der Aufklärung*. Stuttgart: Reclam.

Sturm, Dieter, and Klaus Völker. 1968. *Von denen Vampiren oder Menschensaugern: Dichtungen und Dokumente*. Munich: Carl Hanser.
Thompson, Stith. 1956. *Motif-Index of Folk-Literature*. Copenhagen: Centraltrykkeriet.
Trainer, James. 1964. *Ludwig Tieck: From Gothic to Romantic*. The Hague: Mouton.
Trombley, Frank R. 1994. *Hellenic Religion and Christianization: c. 370–529*. New York: Leiden.
Trunz, Erich. 1988. *Goethe—Gedichte*. Munich: C.H. Beck.
Volckmann, Silvia. 1987. "'Gierig saugt sie seines Mundes Flammen.' Anmerkungen zum Funktionswandel des weiblichen Vampirs in der Literatur des 19. Jahrhunderts." In *Weiblichkeit und Tod in der Literatur,* edited by Renate Berger and Inge Stephan, 155–76. Cologne: Böhlau.
Weidhorn, Manfred. 1988. "Dream." In *Dictionary of Literary Themes and Motifs*, edited by Jean-Charles Seigneuret, 406–13. Westport, CT: Greenwood Press.
Wirsich-Irwin, Gabriele. 1992. *Die deutsche Literatur: Ein Abriß in Text und Darstellung—Klassik*. Stuttgart: Reclam.
Wolf, Leonard. 1975. *The Annotated Dracula.* New York: Crown Publishers.

Index

aristocratic: corruption, 26; vampire, 31, 63, 71n26, 85, 96, 101
Arnod Paole, 4, 23, 82. *See also* folktale; *Visum et repertum*
Austria, 2, 11, 29, 70n11, 99, 100; Austrian, xii, 2, 4, 100. *See also* Charles VI; *The Mysterious Stranger*; Wachsmann, Karl Adolf von
Austro-Hungarian Empire, 34, 70n11. *See also* Charles VI; Habsburg; Maria Theresa

black magic, 75, 78. *See also* Tieck, Ludwig; witchcraft
blood, xiii, xiv, xviiin2, 5, 8, 9, 11, 27, 28, 45, 48, 50, 70n12, 76, 78, 81, 91, 92, 93, 95, 96–97, 100, 119
The Bride of Corinth, xvi, 21, 49–50, 51, 53, 56, 57, 60, 91, 105. *See also* Goethe, Johann Wolfgang von
Bürger, Gottfried August, xii, xvi, xviiin1, 16, 21, 28, 29–31, 32, 33–34, 35–36, 37, 38, 39, 42, 46, 53, 59, 61, 66–67, 71n23, 93–94, 105. *See also Lenore*
burial, 7, 11, 19n6, 19n7; practices, 11
Burke, Edmund, 58, 78, 104, 105

Calmet, Dom Augustin, 10–11
cannibalism, 17, 73, 74, 85, 86, 102n4. *See also* cannibalistic
cannibalistic, 9, 86. *See also* cannibalism

Carniola Mountains, 99. *See also* Carpathian Mountains; *The Mysterious Stranger*; Slovenia; Wachsmann, Karl Adolf von
Carpathian Mountains, 73, 99. *See also* Carniola Mountains; *The Mysterious Stranger*; Slovenia; Wachsmann, Karl Adolf von
cemetery, 41, 42, 43, 76, 78, 83, 84, 86. *See also* graveyard
central Europe, 2, 4, 5, 9, 10–11, 16–17, 21, 22, 23, 24, 25, 27–28, 35, 41, 73, 86. *See also* central European folklore; central European vampire
central European folklore, xii, 4, 8–9, 17, 40–41, 45–46, 66, 71n25, 103. *See also* central Europe; central European vampire
central European vampire, xii, xvi, 2–4, 12, 14, 18, 73, 93. *See also* central Europe; central European folklore; vampire superstition
Charles VI, Emperor, xii, xiv, xvi, 2, 5, 12, 13, 18, 22, 23, 25, 68, 101. *See also* Austria; Austrian; Austro-Hungarian Empire; Habsburg; Maria Theresa
Christabel, 21, 30, 46, 70n18, 71n23, 71n24, 71n26. *See also* Coleridge, Samuel Taylor
Christian, 7, 16, 24, 26, 27–28, 35, 39, 48, 49, 53, 54, 55–56, 66–67, 68, 69n7. *See*

126　Index

also Christianity
Christianity, 24, 25, 26, 27–28, 47, 49, 50, 53, 54–56, 57, 67, 78. *See also* Christian
coffin, 8, 14–16, 44, 45, 46, 58, 60, 62, 64
The Cold Sweetheart, xvi, 21, 60, 61, 64, 67. *See also* Eichendorff, Joseph von
Coleridge, Samuel Taylor, xiii, 21, 30, 46, 70n18, 71n23, 71n24, 71n26. *See also Christabel*
consecrated host, 68. *See also* Eucharist
corpse, xv, 6, 7, 8–10, 19n6, 48, 49, 63, 67, 79, 84, 86, 91, 95, 97, 99, 106
crucifix, 68, 79

decapitation, 5
decomposition, xiv, xviiin2, 5, 6, 7, 10, 18, 19n6, 25
Der Naturforscher, xvi. *See also* Mylius, Christlob; scientific journal
Der Vampir, xii, xvi, xvii, 23, 71n23. *See also* Ossenfelder, Heinrich August
disease, 12, 95. *See also* epidemic; illness
Dracula, xii, 8, 17, 19n9–19n10, 41, 46, 69, 70n15–70n18, 71n24, 73, 94–95, 98–99, 100, 101. *See also* Stoker, Bram

Eichendorff, Joseph von, xvi, 21, 46, 49, 59–60, 61, 63–65, 66, 67, 105–106. *See also The Cold Sweetheart*; *The Late Wedding*
enlightened, 4, 6, 23, 27–28, 56, 67, 68. *See also* Enlightenment
Enlightenment, 1, 2–4, 10, 12, 13, 18, 23, 24, 25. *See also* enlightened
epidemic, 4, 5–6, 8, 45
erotic, 8, 28, 29, 50, 56, 66, 105–106. *See also* eroticism; eroticization; eroticize
eroticism, 28
eroticization, 8, 66, 103. *See also* erotic; eroticism; eroticize
eroticize, 8, 23, 66, 98. *See also* erotic; eroticism; eroticization
Eucharist, 79. *See also* consecrated host
exhume, xviiin2, 5, 6, 7, 11, 17, 68, 81, 93. *See also* exhumation
exhumation, 13, 40. *See also* exhume
explained supernatural, xvii. *See also* supernatural

fairy tale, 8–9, 14–16, 35, 40, 74–75, 76, 87, 94, 102n4. *See also Love Magic*; *The Vampire Princess*; *Wake Not the Dead*
femme fatale, xii, 22, 48–52, 59–60
Flückinger, Johannes, 2–4, 11, 18n2, 23, 25, 82
folklore, xi–xii, xiv, xv, xvi, 2–5, 6, 7, 8–9, 14, 16–18, 22, 27–28, 30, 33, 35–36, 40–42, 44, 45–46, 48, 49, 54, 59, 65, 66, 67–68, 86, 93–94, 95, 97, 98, 103; vampire folklore, xii, xv, 7, 17, 55, 65, 66, 71n25, 86, 93. *See also* folktale
folktale, xiv, xvi, 5, 7, 9, 16, 30, 49, 97. *See also* Arnod Paole; folklore; *Peter Plogojowitz*; *The Shoemaker of Silesia*; vampire folktale; *The Vampire Princess*; *Visum et repertum*

garlic, 68
German. *See* German vampire folklore; German vampire literature; German vampire poetry; Germany; Nachzehrer; vampire
German vampire folklore, xv, 14, 65, 66, 86, 93
German vampire literature, xiii, xvi
German vampire poetry, xiv, 67, 69, 71n23
Germany, xii, xvi, xvii, 2, 4, 13, 14, 18, 29, 34, 36, 49, 53, 69n3, 69n6, 73, 87, 91, 96, 101, 104, 106–107
ghost, xiv–xv, 7, 8–9, 10, 14–16, 33, 40, 43, 44–45, 46, 48, 49, 55, 64, 71n30, 81, 104. *See also The Bride of Corinth*; *Lenore*; *The Shoemaker of Silesia*
Goethe, Johann Wolfgang von, xvi, 16, 21, 28–29, 31, 46, 48, 49–50, 51–53, 54–56, 57, 58, 59–60, 63, 66, 67, 70n14, 70n20–71n23, 71n26, 91, 94, 96, 105, 107
Gothic, 30, 58, 78, 83, 102n6, 104, 106–107; dread, 58, 106; horror, xii–xiii, xvi–xvii, 87, 91, 92, 103, 104, 106, 107; novel, xiii; sublime, 78
grave, xiv, xv, xvi, 8, 14–16, 32, 33, 40–41, 42, 50, 58, 60, 67, 79, 81, 91, 93, 97
graveyard, 42, 57, 58, 97. *See also* cemetery

Index

Greece, 2, 5, 53, 78. *See also* Greek; vrykolakas
Greek, 5, 6, 7, 9, 14, 31, 41, 46, 49, 69n2, 70n12, 71n24, 79, 94. *See also* Greece; vrykolakas

Habsburg, 2, 12–13, 18, 99–101; Charles VI, xvi, 2, 101; wars against Ottoman Empire, 2, 13, 18, 99–100, 101
Haining, Peter, xvii, 87, 88, 89, 102n6. *See also* Tieck, Ludwig; *Wake Not the Dead*
Hildebrandt, Theodor, xvii, 73, 97–98. *See also* Russian vampire; *The Vampire or the Bride of Death*
Hoffmann, E. T. A., xiii, xvi, xvii, 57, 73, 75, 80–82, 83, 85–86, 92, 93, 102n4, 103, 105–106. *See also Vampirismus*
holy water, 68, 79
horror: aesthetic of, 78; literature, xii–xiii, xvi–xvii, 57, 85, 87, 91, 92, 103, 104, 106, 107; poetry, 23; sublime aesthetic, 58
Hungary, xvi, 2, 10, 11, 13–14, 18, 24–25, 27, 32, 35, 41, 69n6, 81, 99

illness, 5, 8–9, 47, 55, 77, 79, 99. *See also* disease; epidemic

Kant, Immanuel, 57–58, 78, 105

The Late Wedding, 21, 59, 62, 63–64. *See also* Eichendorff, Joseph von
Lenore, xii, xvi, 14, 16–17, 21, 29–31, 32, 33–34, 35–37, 38–42, 43–45, 53, 61, 71n23, 73, 93–94, 106. *See also* Bürger, Gottfried August
Love Magic, xvii, 73, 74–75, 79. *See also* Tieck, Ludwig

Maria Theresa, Empress, 13, 34. *See also* Austro-Hungarian; Charles VI; Seven Years' War; witchcraft
Murnau, Friedrich Wilhelm, 1, 46. *See also Nosferatu*
Mylius, Christlob, 4, 23–24, 25. *See also Der Naturforscher*; scientific journal
The Mysterious Stranger, xvii, 98. *See also* Wachsmann, Karl Adolf von

Nachzehrer, xvi, 14, 17, 19n8, 73
necrophilia, 14, 17, 27, 35, 48, 65, 66, 74, 85–86, 93. *See also The Bride of Corinth*; German vampire folklore; *The Late Wedding*; *Lenore*; *Vampirismus*; *Wake Not the Dead*
Nosferatu, 1, 46. *See also* Murnau, Friedrich Wilhelm

Ossenfelder, Heinrich August, xii, xiii, xvi, 4, 17–18, 21, 22, 23–24, 25–26, 28–29, 35, 36, 53, 66, 67, 69n3, 69n6, 71n23, 103, 105. *See also Der Vampir*
Ottoman Empire, xvi, 2, 18, 99–100, 101; Turks, xvi, 2, 18. *See also* Austro-Hungarian Empire; Charles VI; Habsburg

Peter Plogojowitz, 4, 5, 8–9. *See also* folktale; Serbia
Poe, Edgar Allan, xiii, 75, 106

Ranft, Michael, 9–10, 81, 82. *See also* scientific
Raupach, Ernst Benjamin Salomo, xvii, 73, 87–88, 89, 90–91, 92–95, 97–98, 102n5, 105–106, 107. *See also Wake Not the Dead*
revenant, xiii, xiv–xv, 5, 6, 7, 9, 10, 14, 16, 27, 35, 36, 45, 48, 51, 53, 54, 58, 59–60, 66, 92
Romania, 4, 5, 7–9, 14, 16, 17, 25, 35, 99. *See also* folktale; *The Vampire Princess*
Rousseau, Jean Jacques, 1, 10, 12, 90
Russian vampire, 97. *See also* Hildebrandt, Theodor; *The Vampire or the Bride of Death*

Schiller, Friedrich, xiii, 33–34, 46
science, 4, 10, 12, 25, 36, 51, 52
scientific, xvi, 2–4, 11, 13, 18, 22–23, 24, 25, 36, 68, 82
scientific journal, xvi, 18, 25. *See also Der Naturforscher*; Mylius, Christlob
scientists, xi, xiv, 2–4, 6, 9, 12, 14, 22, 25, 46, 68, 101
Serbia, 2–4, 5–6, 9, 14, 18, 24–25, 35. *See also* folktale; *Peter Plogojowitz*

Seven Years' War, 35, 36, 70n11. *See also* Bürger, Gottfried August; *Lenore*; Maria Theresa

The Shoemaker of Silesia, xiv, 5, 7, 8. *See also* folktale; Silesia

Silesia, xiv, 5, 7, 9, 10, 11, 13, 70n11, 70n19, 90, 99. *See also* folktale; *The Shoemaker of Silesia*

Slavic, 6, 7, 14; folklore, 6, 7, 97

sleep, 6, 7, 26, 27–28, 48, 53, 55, 57, 66, 67, 81, 84, 93, 95

Slovenia, 2, 99. *See also* Carniola Mountains; Wachsmann, Karl Adolf von

stake, 11, 45, 81; staking, 5, 6, 53, 100

Stoker, Bram, xii, 8, 17, 41, 46, 64, 67, 69, 70n15–70n18, 71n24, 71n27, 73, 94–95, 98, 100. *See also* Dracula

suicide, 5, 7, 17, 48, 50, 53, 54–55, 67, 97

supernatural, xiii, xvii, 12, 33, 36, 40, 42, 45, 46, 56, 64, 68, 75, 81, 94, 96, 107. *See also* explained supernatural

superstition. *See* vampire superstition

Tieck, Ludwig, xiii, xvi–xvii, 49, 73, 74–75, 76, 78–80, 82, 87–88, 89–90, 92, 95, 102n6, 105–106. *See also Love Magic*

Uhland, Ludwig, 30. *See also* Bürger, Gottfried August; *Lenore*

vampire: Byelorussian, 97; in central European stories, xii, xvi, 4, 14; in central European superstition, 2–4, 12, 14, 18, 73, 93; debates, 10, 22, 25, 53, 82; folkloric, xii, xiv, 8, 17–18, 41, 45; folktale, xiv, 5, 7; in German folklore, xv, 65, 66, 86, 93; in German literature, xiii, xiv, xvi, 28, 69, 71n23; Russian, 97; superstition, xii, 2–4, 7, 10, 12, 18, 35, 54, 73, 81–82, 93. *See also* folktale; vampire-like; vampiric

The Vampire. See Der Vampir; Ossenfelder, Heinrich August

The Vampire or the Bride of Death, xvii, 97. *See also* Hildebrandt, Theodor; Russian vampire

vampire-like, xvi, 6, 22, 70n12, 73

vampiric, 2–4, 24, 46, 59–60, 71n27

The Vampire Princess, 7–9, 22. *See also* folktale; Romania

Vampirismus, xvi, xvii, 73, 80, 83, 85, 103. *See also* Hoffmann, E. T. A

Visum et repertum, 23, 25, 82. *See also* Arnod Paole; folktale

Voltaire, 10–12

vrykolakas, 4, 5, 6, 7, 70n19, 79. *See also* Greece; Greek

Wachsmann, Karl Adolf von, xvii, 73, 98–99. *See also* Austria; Habsburg; Carniola Mountains; *The Mysterious Stranger*

Wake Not the Dead, xvii, 73, 87–88, 89–90, 91, 95, 97, 102n6, 106. *See also* fairy tale; Haining, Peter; Raupach, Ernst Benjamin Salomo

witchcraft, 13, 78–79. *See also* black magic; Maria Theresa, Empress; Tieck, Ludwig

About the Author

Heide Crawford teaches German language, literature, and culture in the Department of Germanic & Slavic Studies at the University of Georgia.